Matuseski

JOY TO THE WORLD

CONTENTS

— PIANO LEVEL —
LATE ELEMENTARY/EARLY INTERMEDIATE
(HLSPL LEVEL 3-4)

ISBN 0-634-04747-7

7777 W. BLUEMOUND RD. P.O. BOX 13819 MILWAUKEE, WI 53213

In Australia Contact: HAL LEONARD AUSTRALIA Pty. Ltd.
22 Taunton Drive P.O. Box 5130
Cheltenham East, 3192 Victoria, Australia
Email: **ausadmin@halleonard.com**

Visit Hal Leonard Online at
www.halleonard.com

ANGELS WE HAVE HEARD ON HIGH

Traditional French Carol
Translated by JAMES CHADWICK
Arranged by Phillip Keveren

D G

And the moun - tains in re - ply
Say what may the tid - ings be,

mp

Ech - o back their joy - ous strains.
Which in - spire your heav'n - ly song?

E7 Am D7 G C

Glo - - -

mf

D G

- ri - a in ex - cel - sis

D G E7 Am D7
De - o, Glo - -
f
G C D G
- - ri - a in ex - cel - sis
cresc.
1.
D G
De - o.
ff
p
2.
D G
De - o.
rit.
ff

AWAY IN A MANGER

Traditional
Words by JOHN T. McFARLAND (v.3)
Music by JAMES R. MURRAY
Arranged by Phillip Keveren

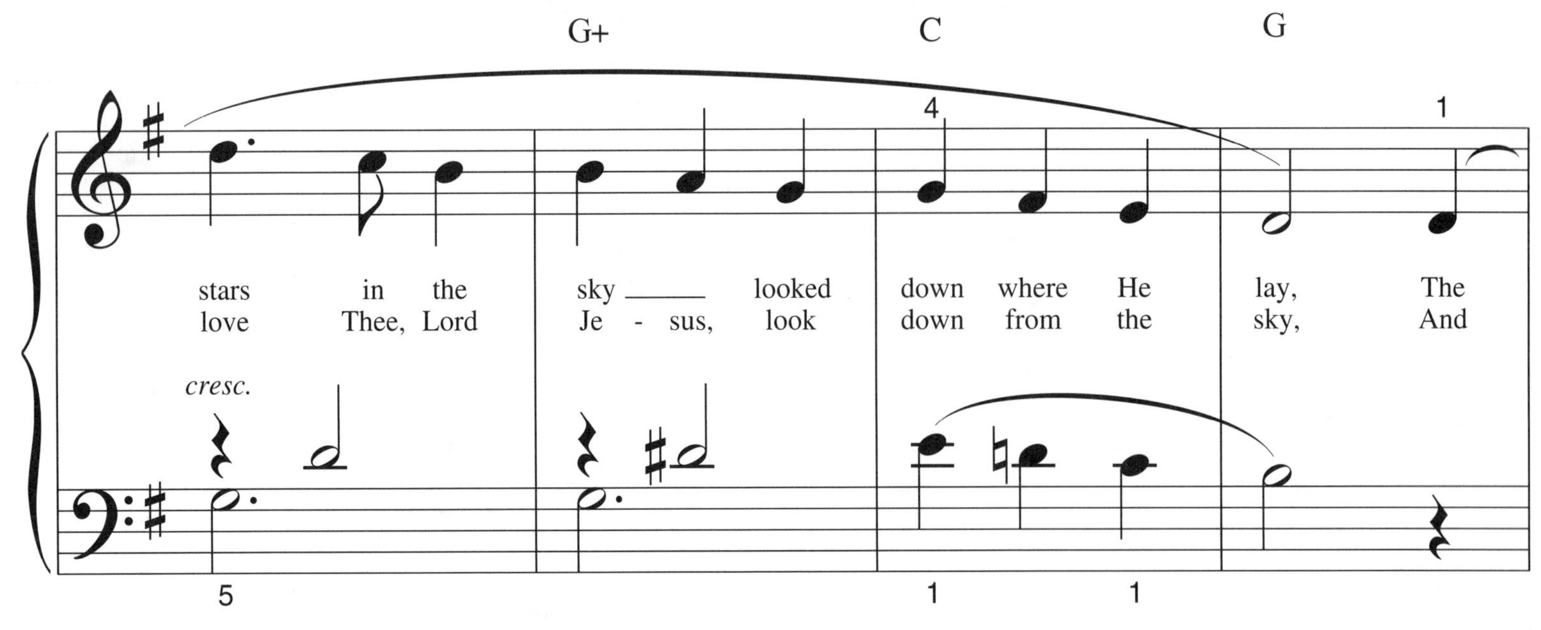
G+
C
G
stars in the sky looked down where He lay, The
love Thee, Lord Je - sus, look down from the sky, And
cresc.

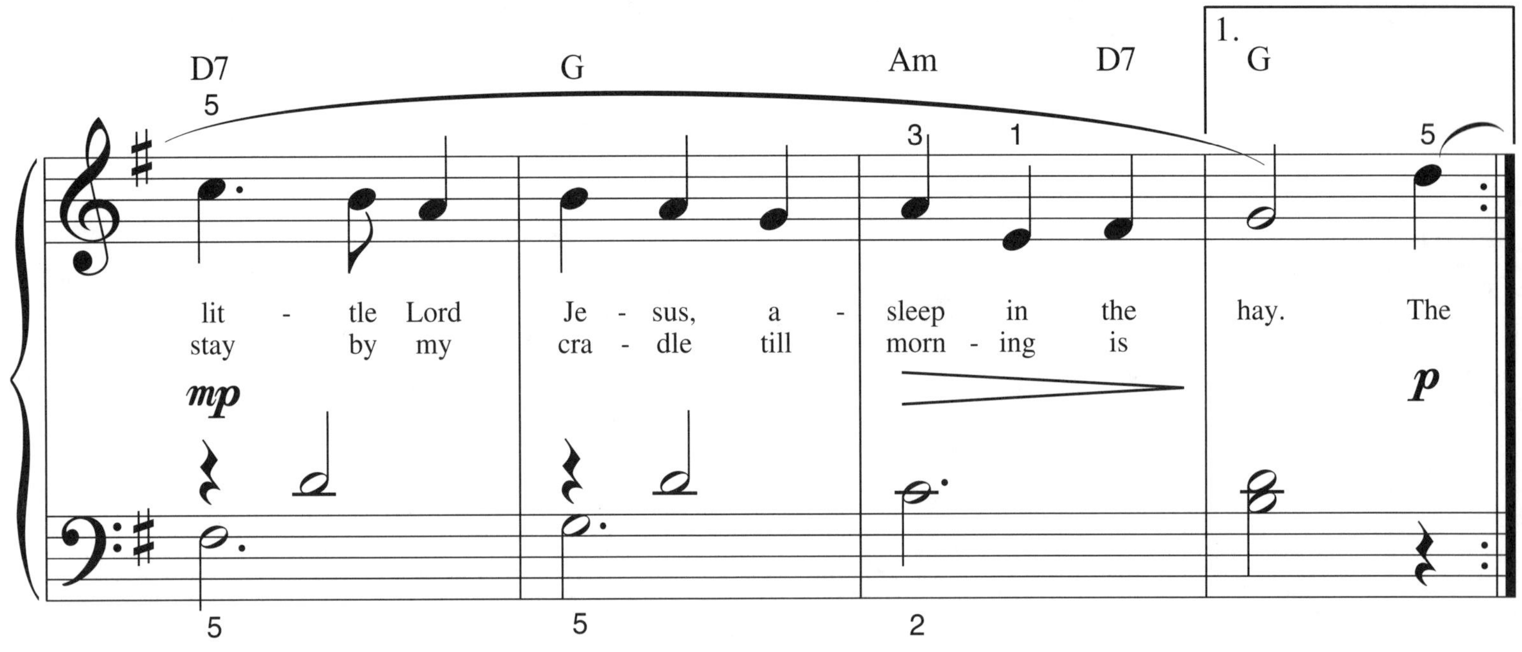
D7
G
Am
D7
1.
G
lit - tle Lord Je - sus, a - sleep in the hay. The
stay by my cra - dle till morn - ing is
mp
p

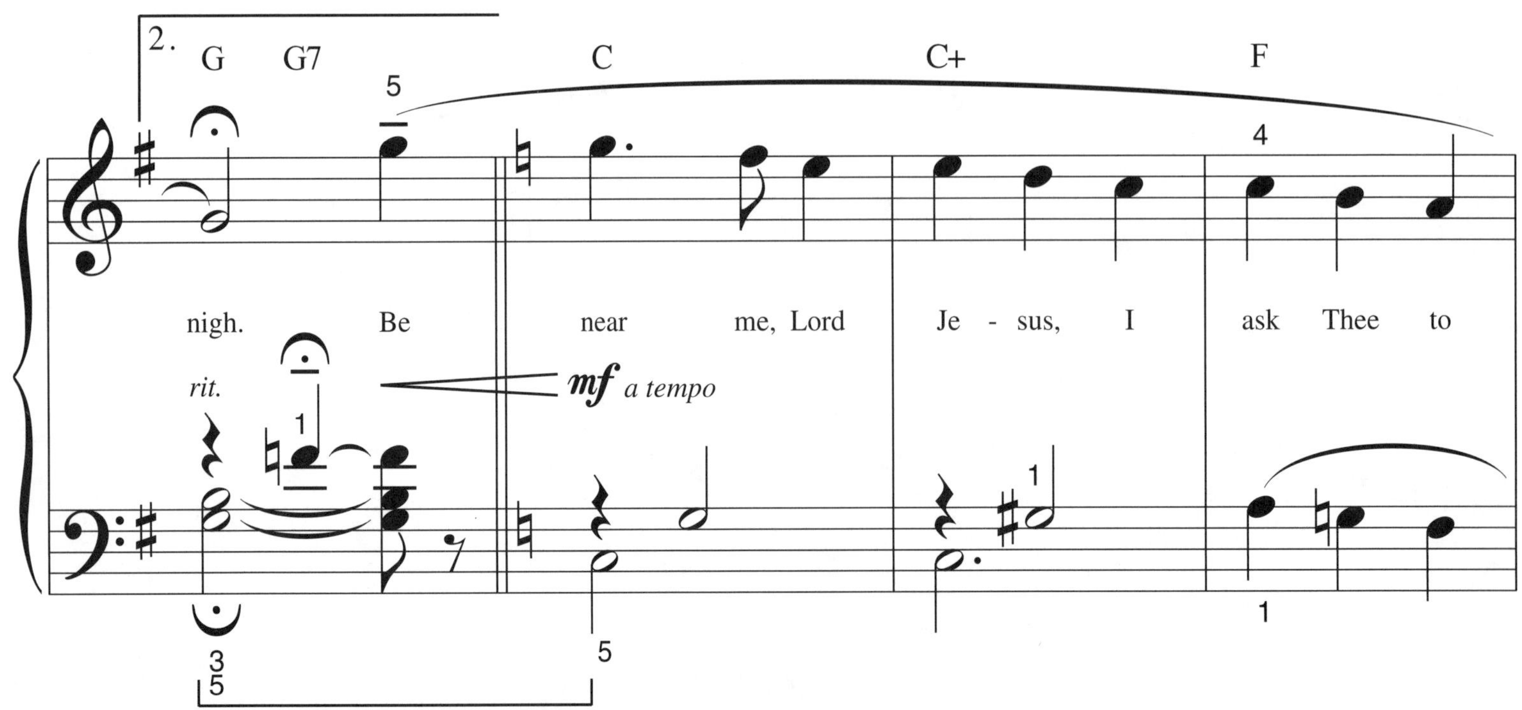
2.
G
G7
C
C+
F
nigh. Be near me, Lord Je - sus, I ask Thee to
rit.
mf a tempo

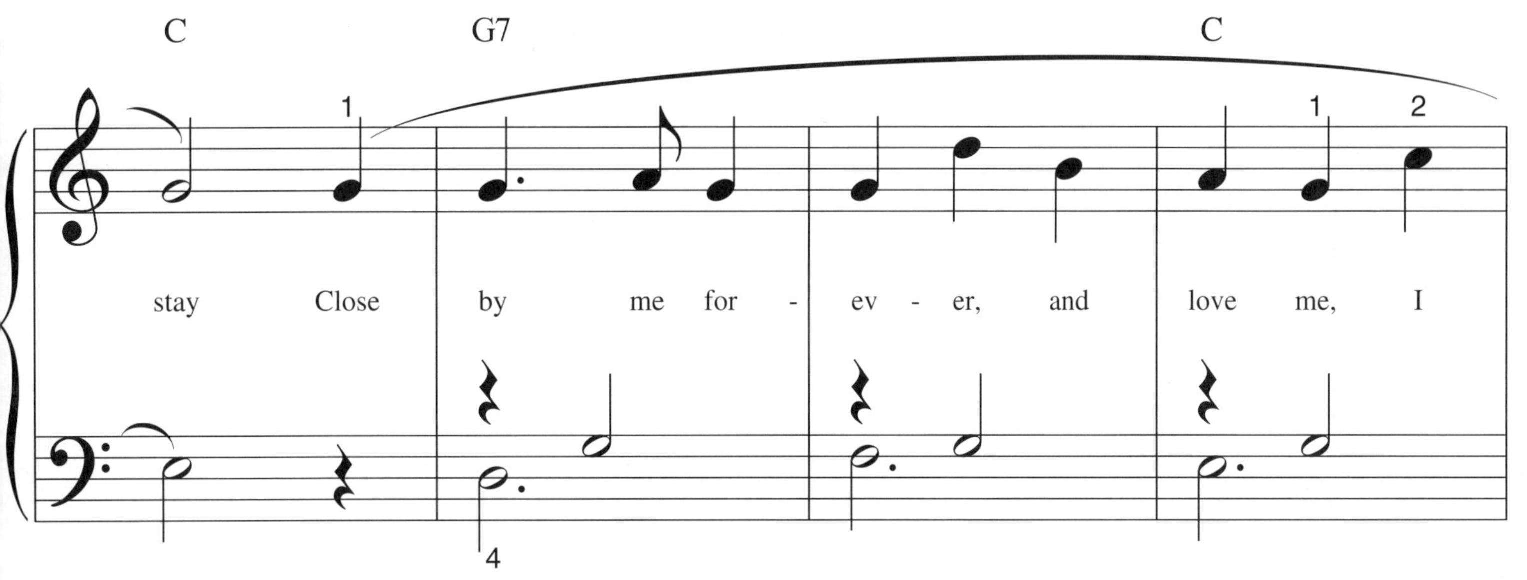
C
G7
C
stay Close by me for - ev - er, and love me, I

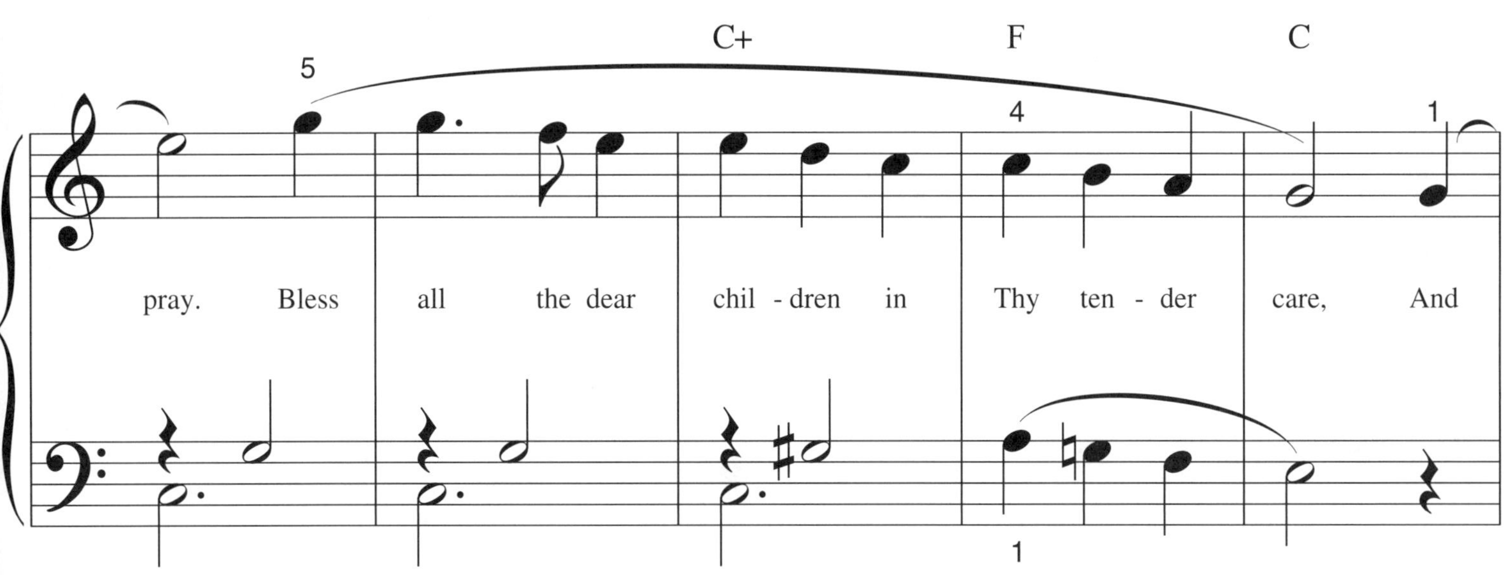
C+
F
C
pray. Bless all the dear chil - dren in Thy ten - der care, And

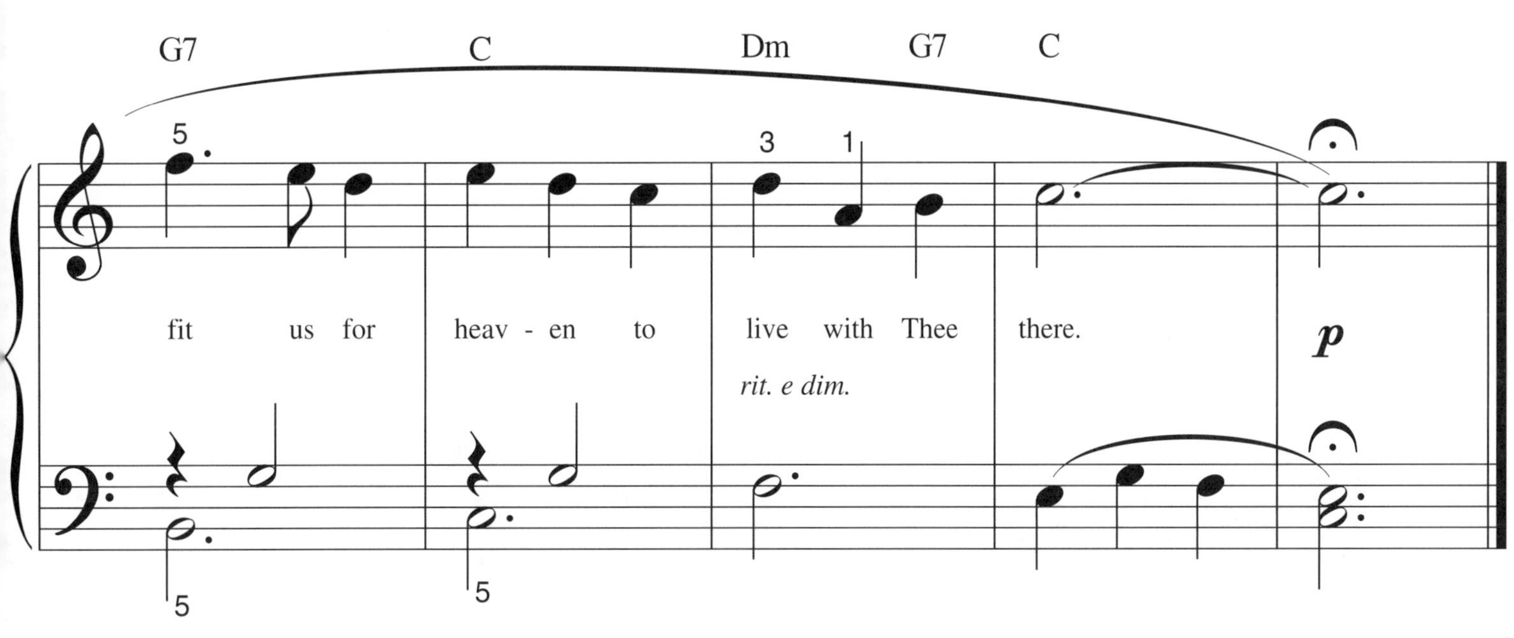
G7
C
Dm
G7
C
fit us for heav - en to live with Thee there.
rit. e dim.

DECK THE HALL

Traditional Welsh Carol
Arranged by Phillip Keveren

C
Am
D7
G7
C5
Fa la la la la la la,
Troll the an - cient
F
C
1.
C/G G7 C
Yule - tide car - ol,
Fa la la la la, la
la la la.
C5
2.
C/G G7
C
C5
la la
la.
B♭sus2
C5

THE FIRST NOEL

17th Century English Carol
Music from W. Sandys' *Christmas Carols*
Arranged by Phillip Keveren

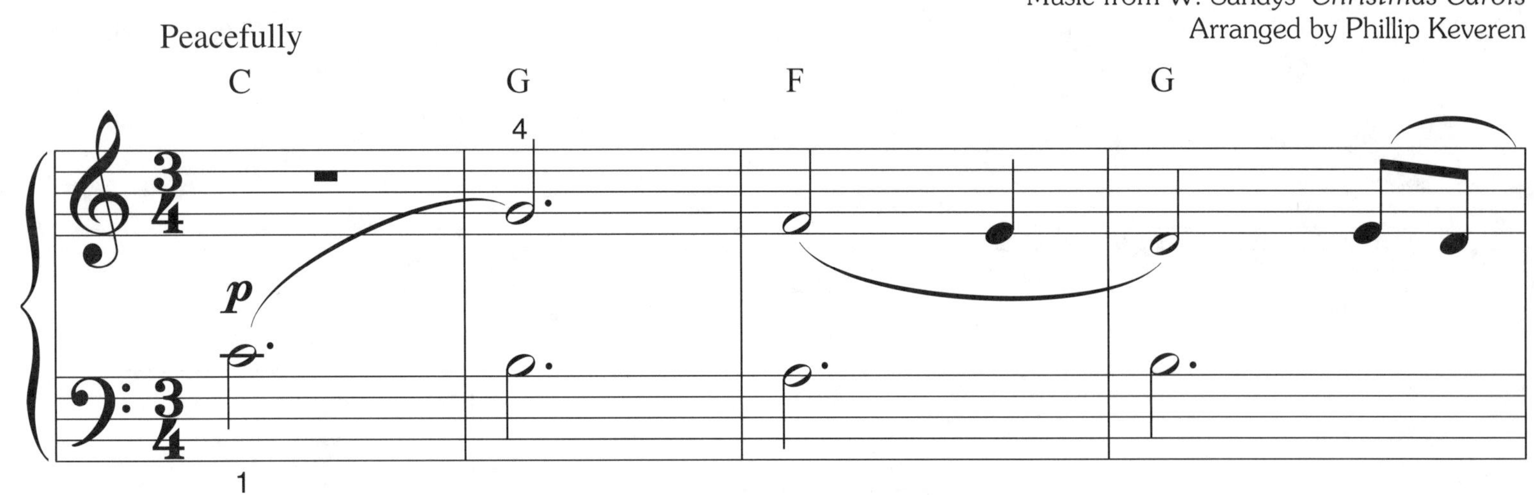

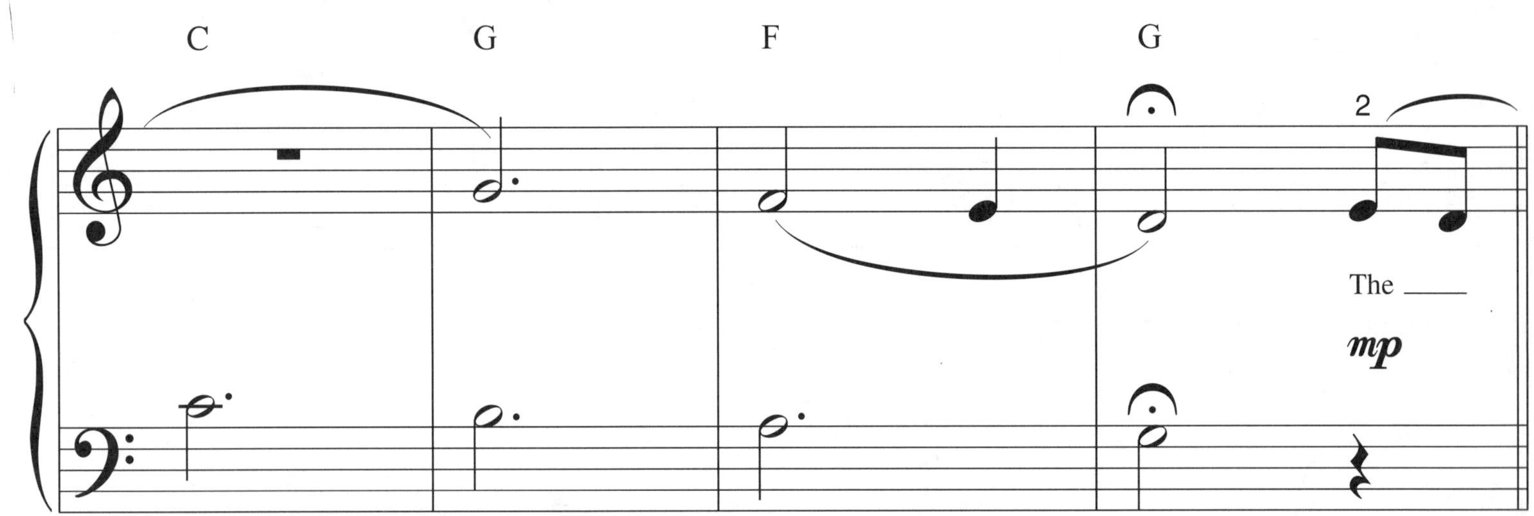

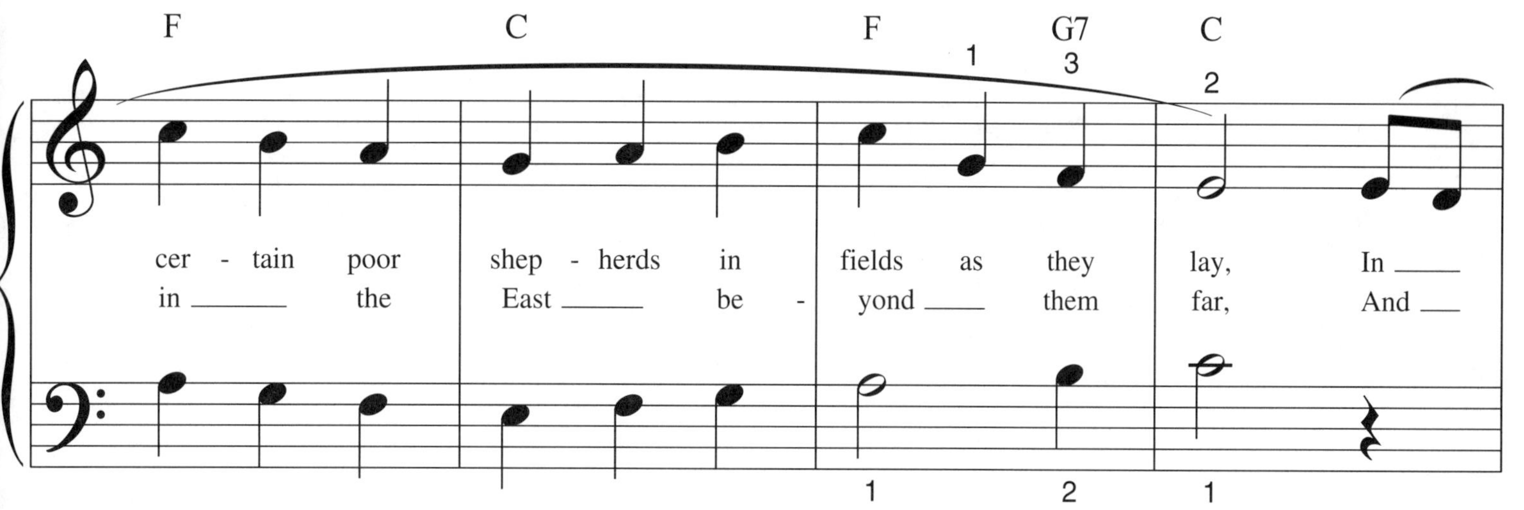
F
C
F
G7
C
cer - tain poor
shep - herds in
fields as they
lay,
In
in the
East be -
yond them
far,
And

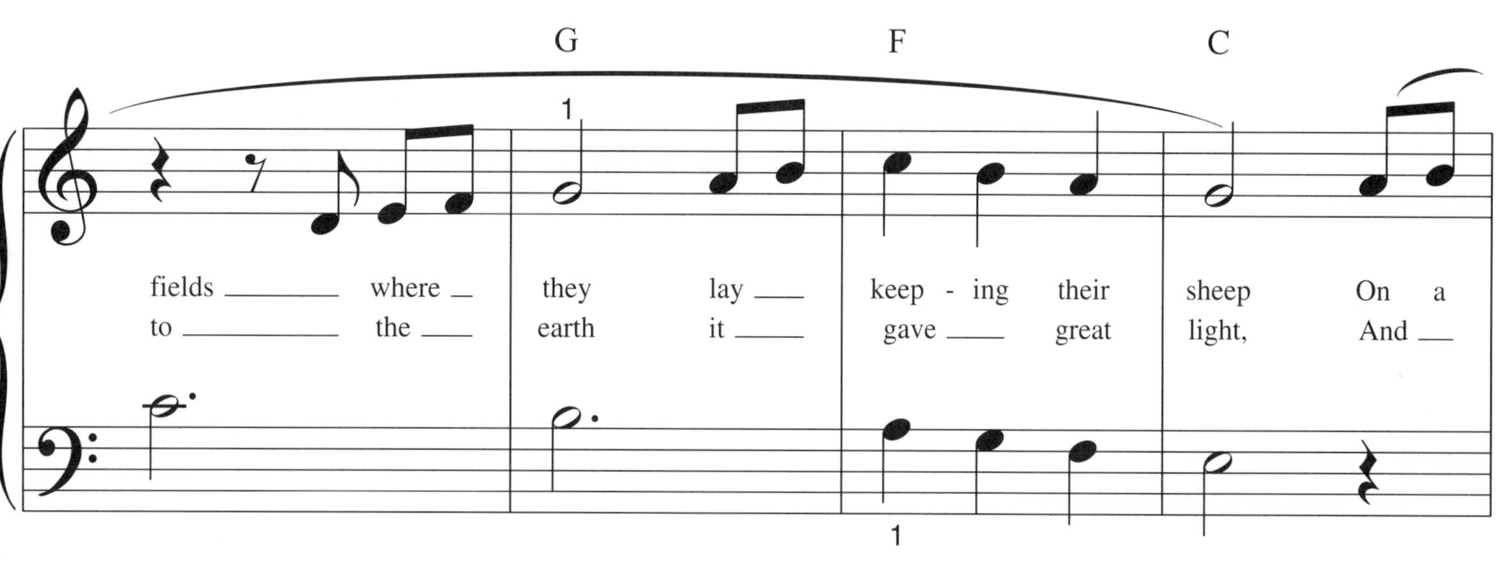
G
F
C
fields where
they lay
keep - ing their
sheep
On a
to the
earth it
gave great
light,
And

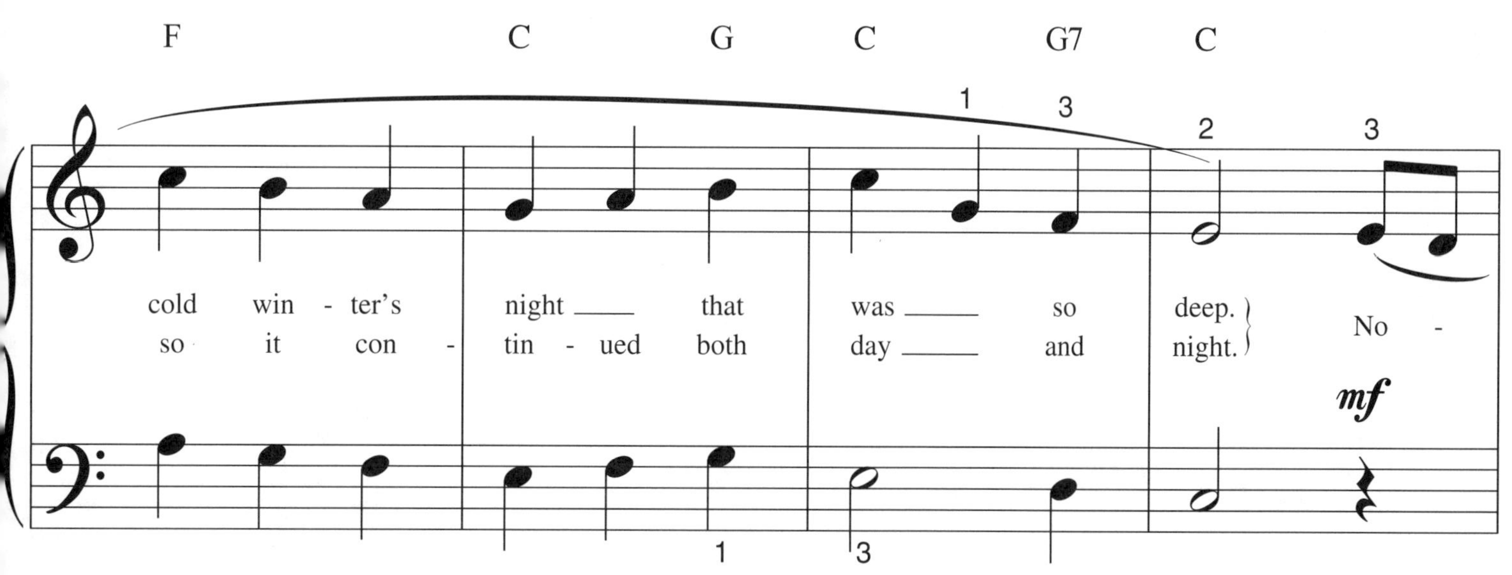
F
C
G
C
G7
C
cold win - ter's
night that
was so
deep.
so it con -
tin - ued both
day and
night.
No -
mf

Em
F
C
1
el, No - el, No - el, No - el.
5
Am
Em
F
G7
1.
C
5
1
2
Born is the King of Is - ra - el. They
mp
1
1
2
1
2.
C
G
F
G
2
4
el.
p
1
C
G
F
G7
C
rit.

IT CAME UPON THE MIDNIGHT CLEAR

Words by EDMUND HAMILTON SEARS
Music by RICHARD STORRS WILLIS
Arranged by Phillip Keveren

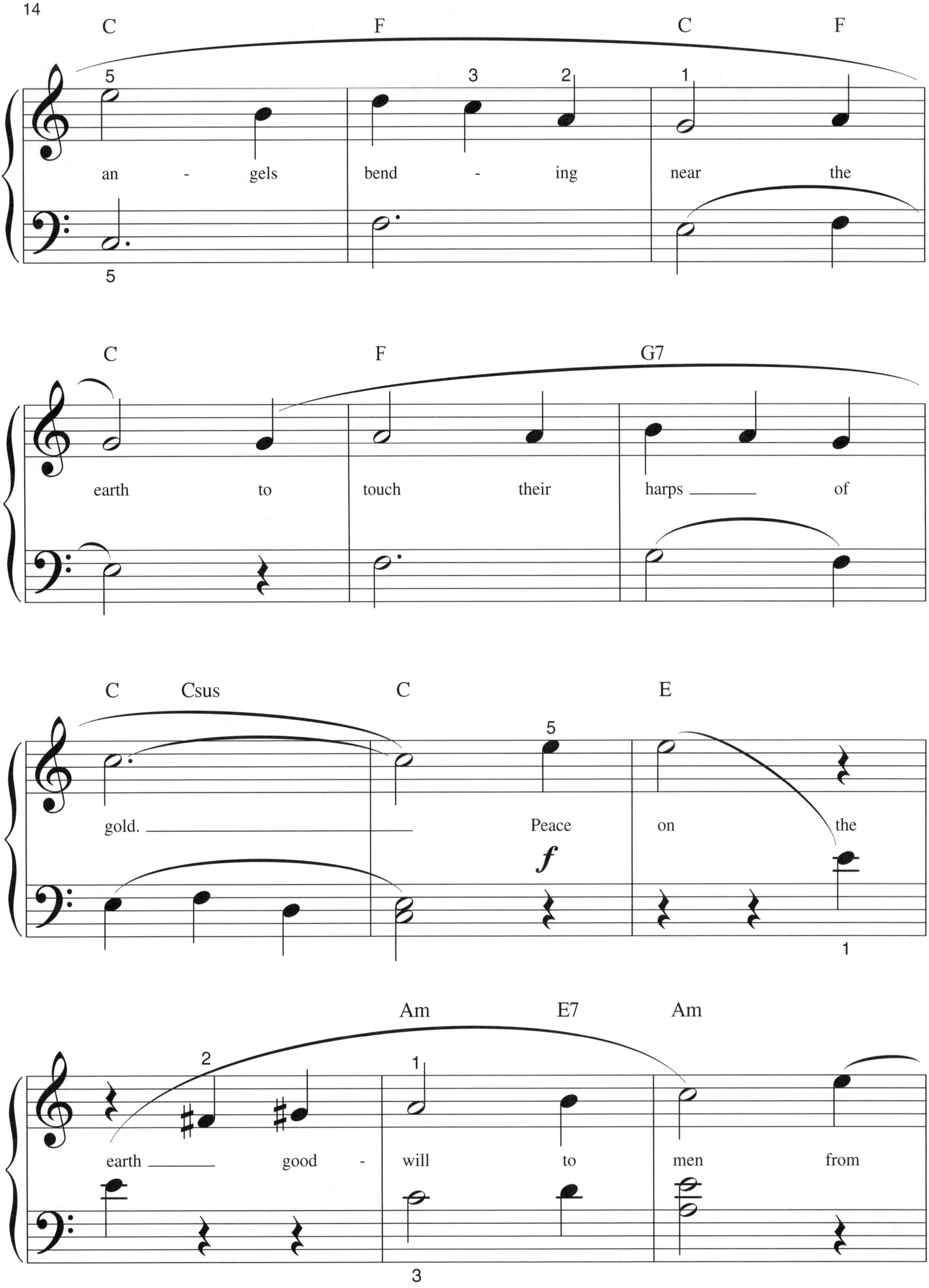
C F C F
an - gels bend - ing near the
C F G7
earth to touch their harps of
C Csus C E
gold. Peace on the
f
Am E7 Am
earth good - will to men from

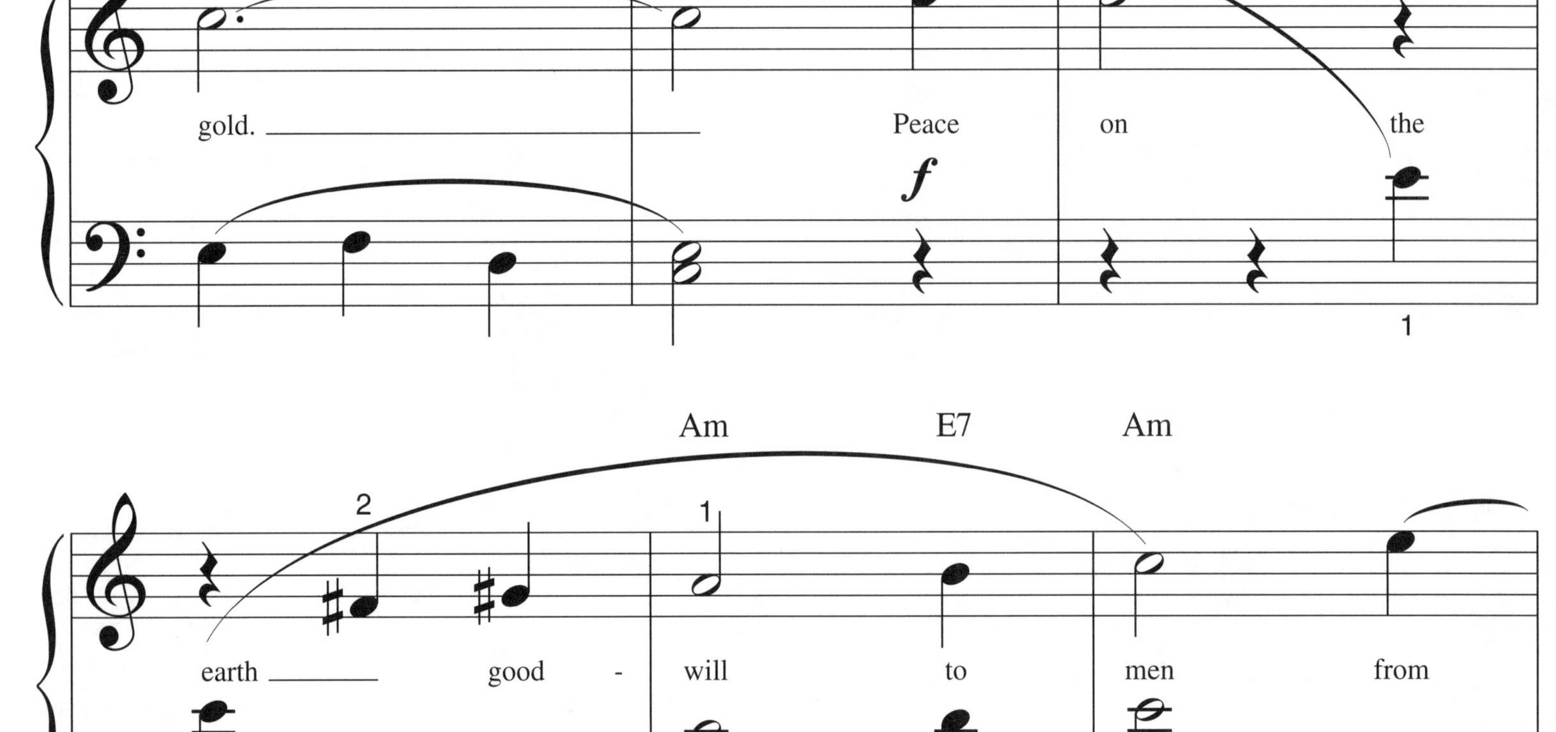

G
D7
G
heav - en's all gra - cious King.
rit.
G7
C
F
The world in sol - emn
mp
a tempo
C
F
C
F
still - ness lay to hear the
Dm
G7
C
an - gels sing.

THE FRIENDLY BEASTS

Traditional English Carol
Arranged by Phillip Keveren

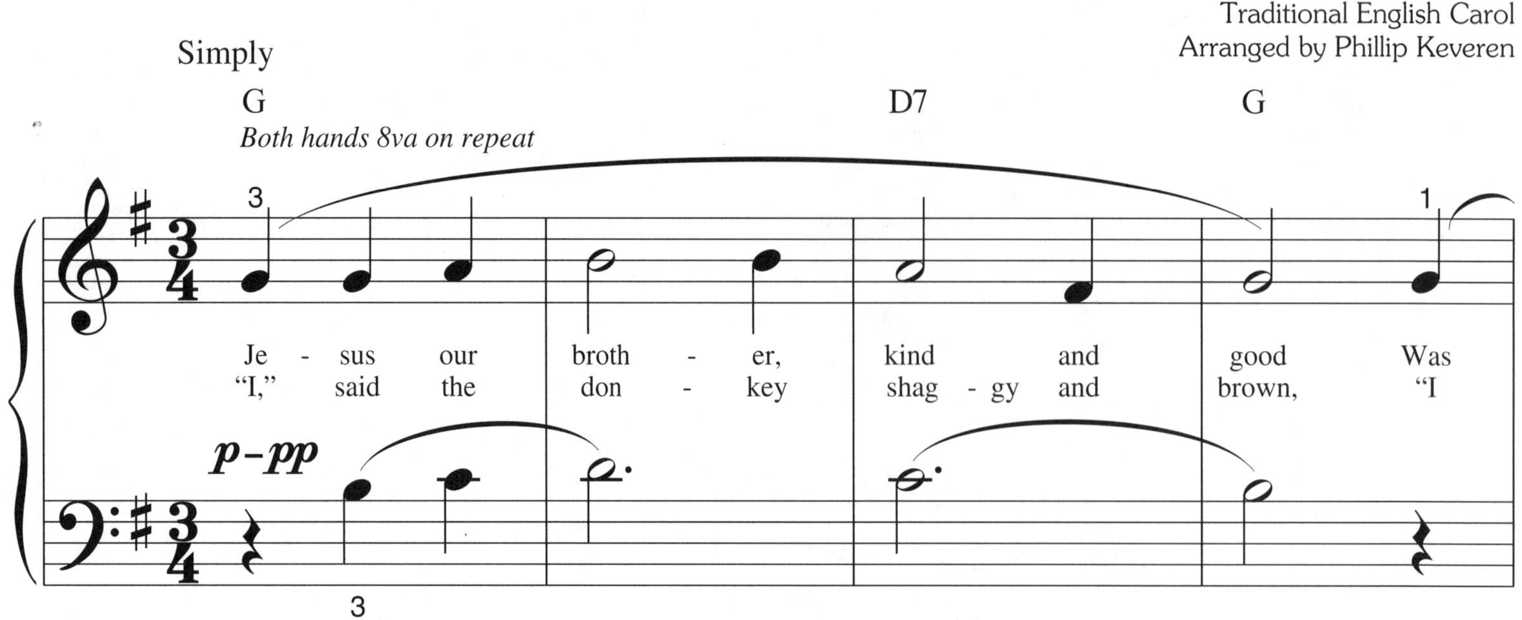

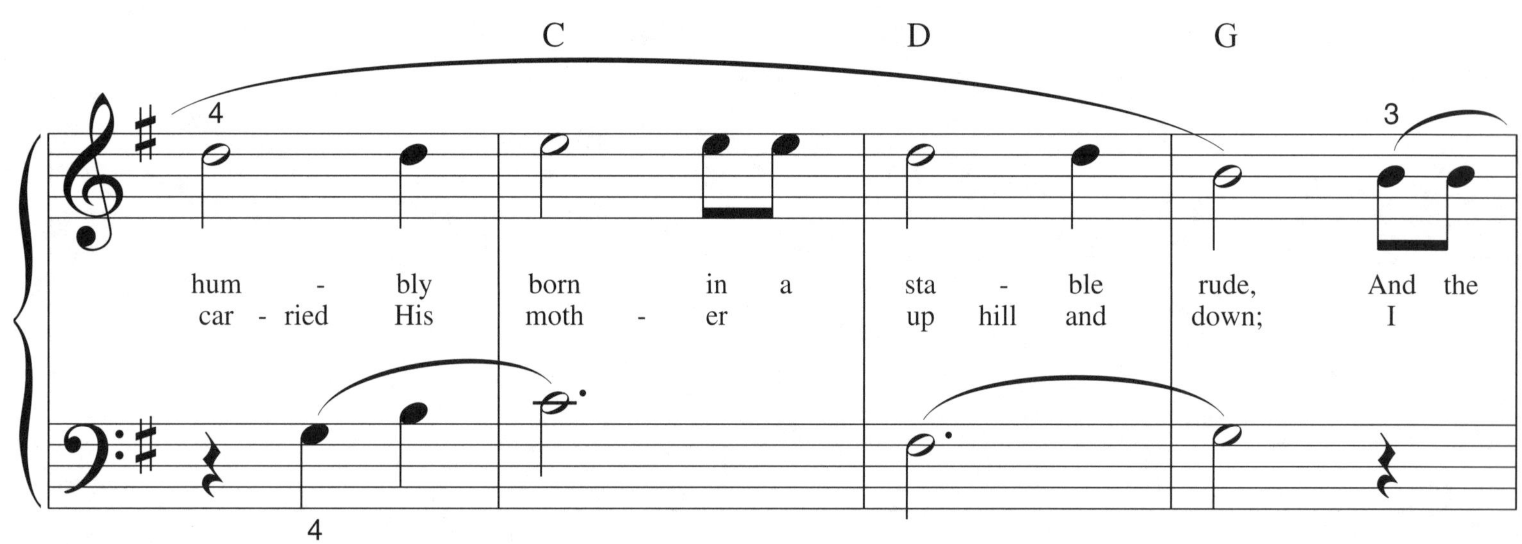

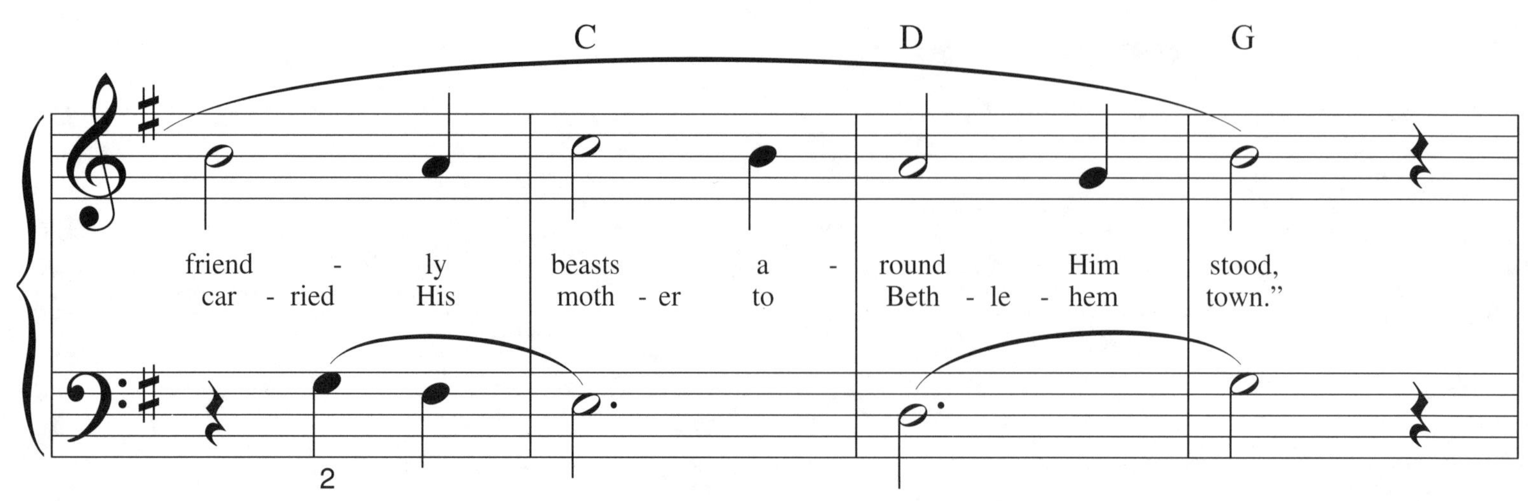

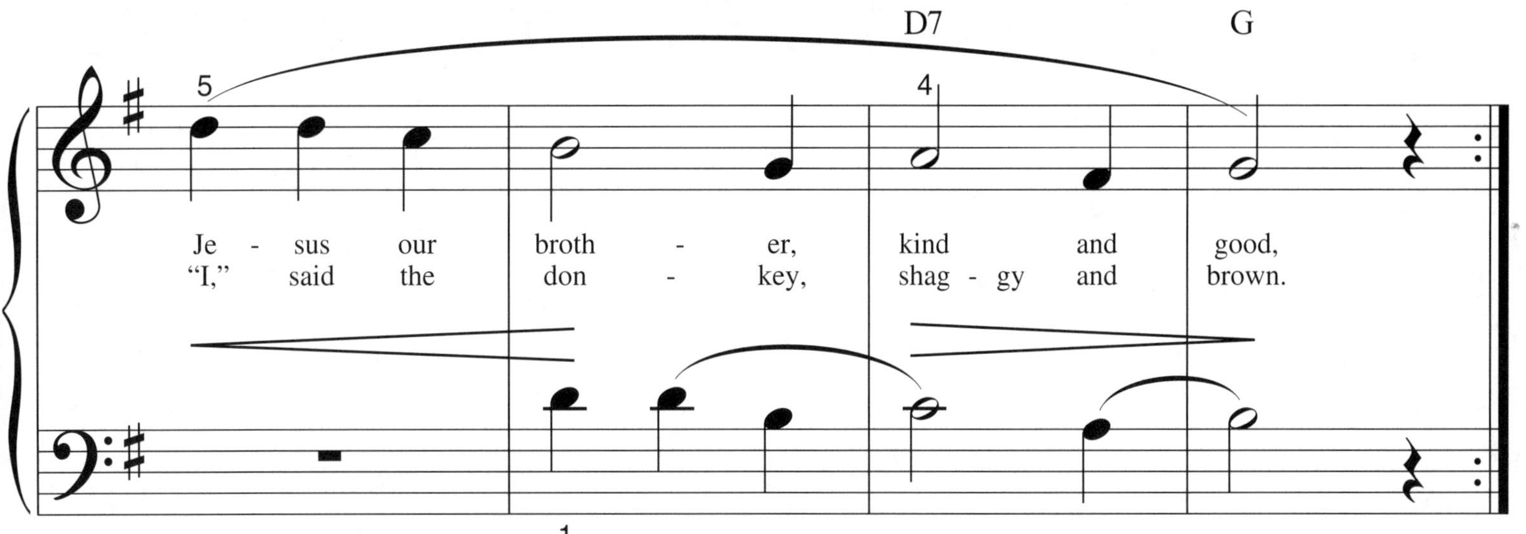

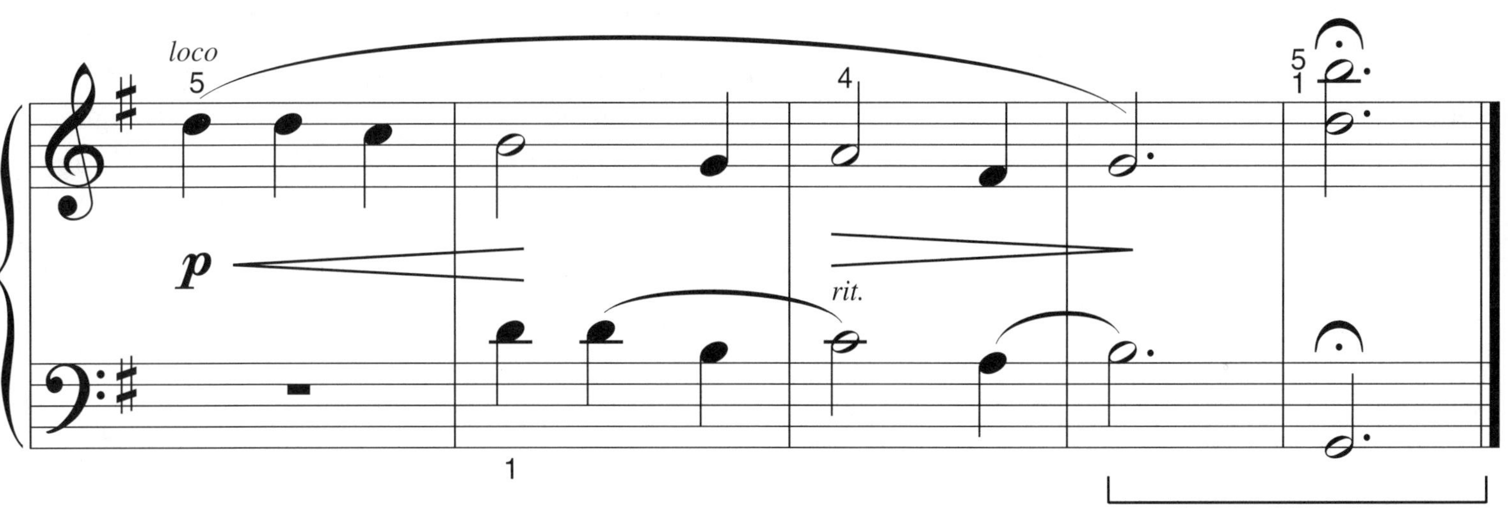

Additional Lyrics

3. "I," said the cow all white and red,
"I gave Him my manger for His bed;
I gave Him my hay to pillow His head."
"I," said the cow all white and red.

4. "I," said the sheep with the curly horn,
"I gave Him my wool for His blanket warm;
He wore my coat on Christmas morn."
"I," said the sheep with the curly horn.

5. "I," said the dove from the rafters high,
"I cooed Him to sleep that He would not cry;
We cooed Him to sleep, my mate and I."
"I," said the dove from the rafters high.

6. Thus every beast by some good spell,
In the stable dark was glad to tell
Of the gift he gave Emmanuel,
The gift he gave Emmanuel.

GOD REST YE MERRY, GENTLEMEN

19th Century English Carol
Arranged by Phillip Keveren

G B7 Em A7 D
Sa - tan's pow'r, When we were gone a - stray;
Mar - y, Did noth - ing take in scorn,
O
mf
G B7 Em D G
tid - ings of com - fort and joy, com - fort and joy, O
poco rit.
f a tempo
1. 2.
B7 Em B7
tid - ings of com - fort and joy. In com - fort and,
p
Em Em6
com - fort and, com - fort and joy.
p
f
pp

HARK! THE HERALD ANGELS SING

Words by CHARLES WESLEY
Altered by GEORGE WHITEFIELD
Music by FELIX MENDELSSOHN-BARTHOLDY
Arranged by WILLIAM H. CUMMINGS
Arranged by Phillip Keveren

Triumphantly

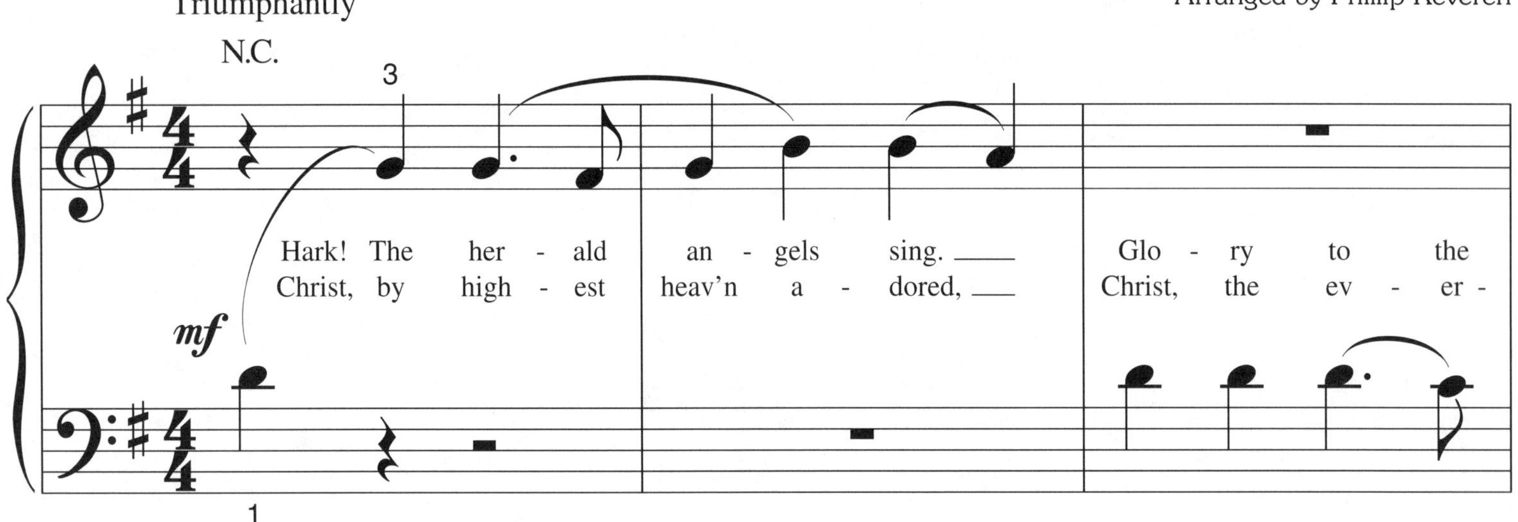

D7 G D
G
D7 G D
na - tions rise,
God - head see:
Join the tri - umph
Hail th'In - car - nate
of the skies;
De - i - ty,
f
mp
C E7
Am E7 Am
D7 G
With th'an - gel - ic
Pleased as Man with
host pro - claim,
man to dwell,
Christ is born in
Je - sus our Em -
mf
D7 G
C E7
Am E7 Am
Beth - le - hem.
man - u - el!
Hark! The her - ald
an - gels sing,
f
D7 G
1.
D7 G
2.
G D7
G
Glo - ry to the
new - born King.
new - born
King.
rit.

JOY TO THE WORLD

Words by ISAAC WATTS
Music by GEORGE FRIDERIC HANDEL
Arranged by LOWELL MASON
Arranged by Phillip Keveren

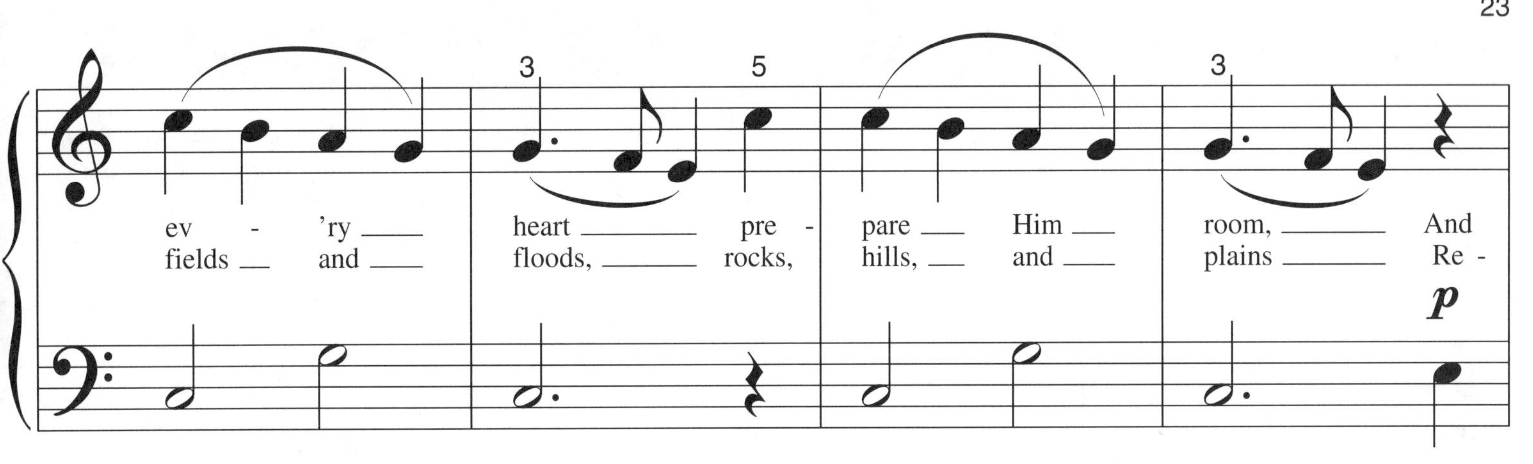
3
5
3
ev - 'ry heart pre - pare Him room, And
fields and floods, rocks, hills, and plains Re -
p

G7
1
heav'n and na - ture sing, And heav'n and na - ture sing, And
peat the sound - ing joy, Re - peat the sound - ing joy, Re -
mp
f

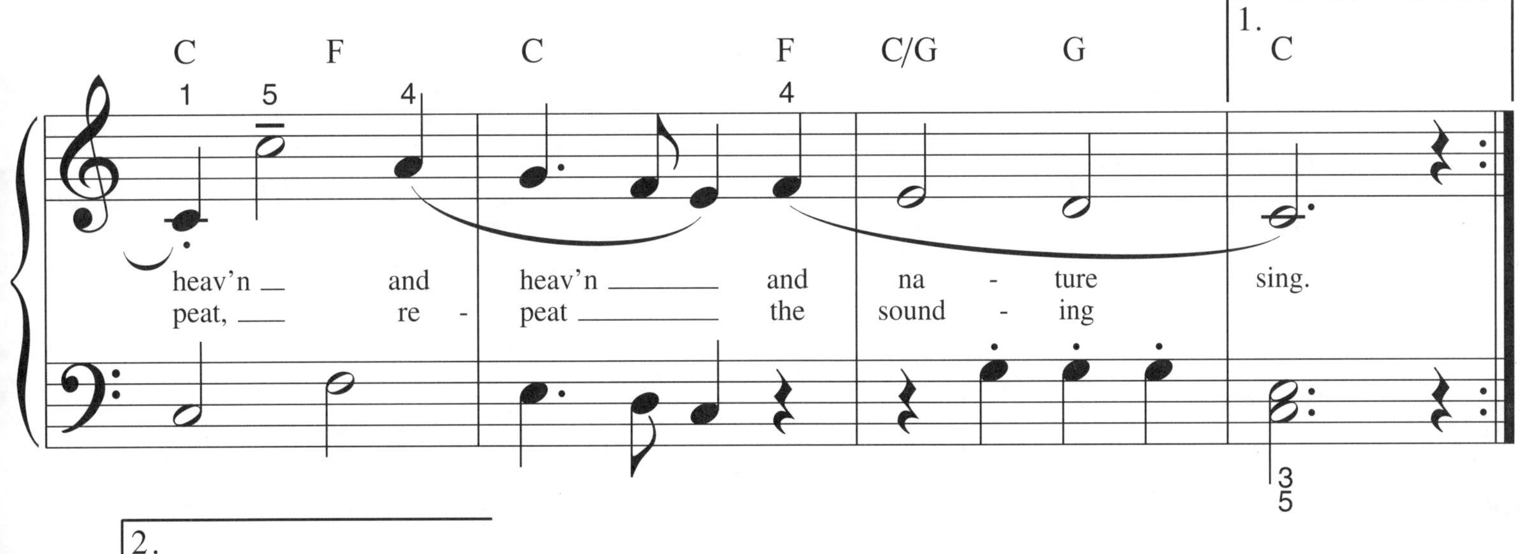
C F C F C/G G
1. C
1 5 4 4
heav'n and heav'n and na - ture sing.
peat, re - peat the sound - ing
3
5

2.
C
1
5
1
joy.
ff

LO, HOW A ROSE E'ER BLOOMING

15th Century German Carol
Translated by THEODORE BAKER
Music from *Alte Catholische Geistliche Kirchengesang*
Arranged by Phillip Keveren

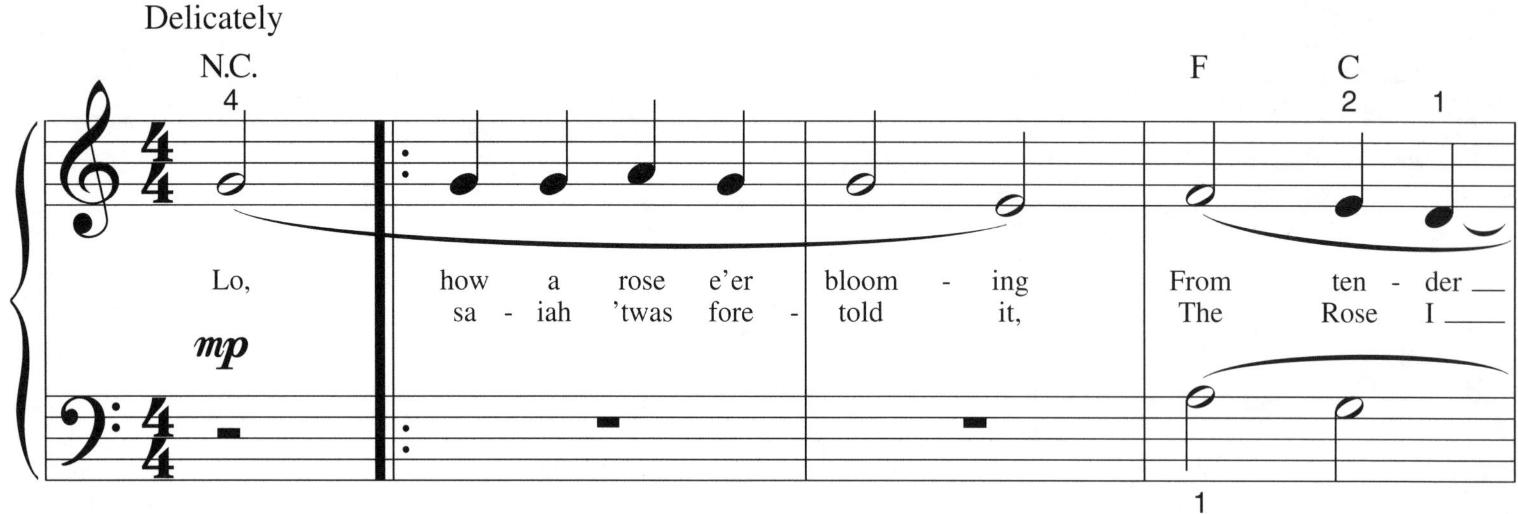

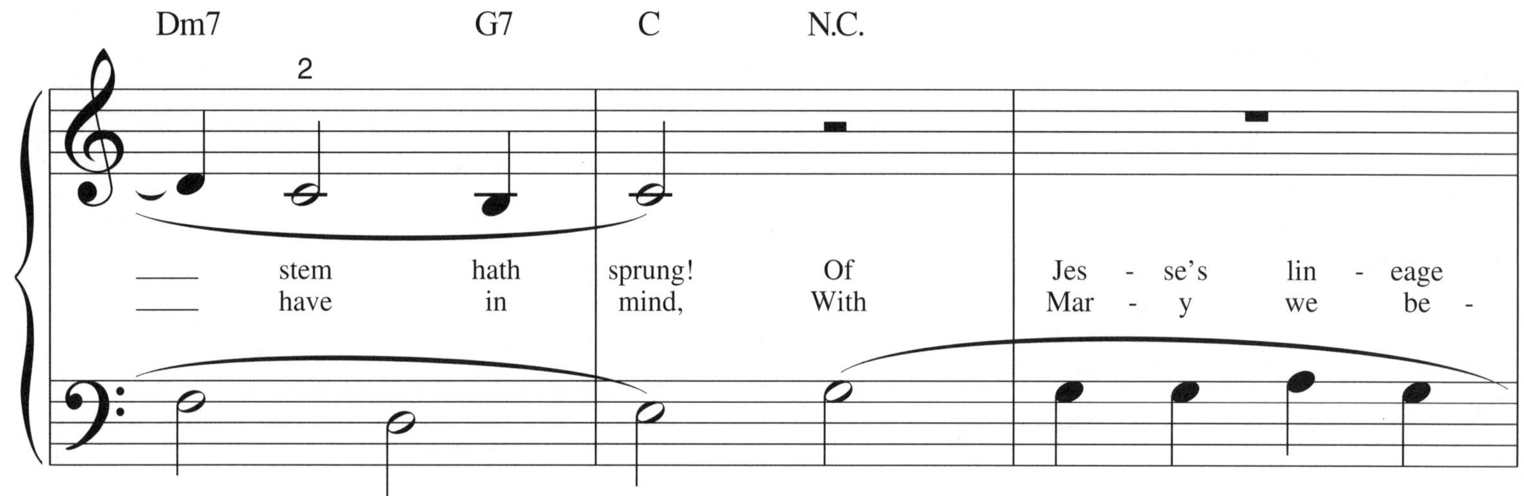

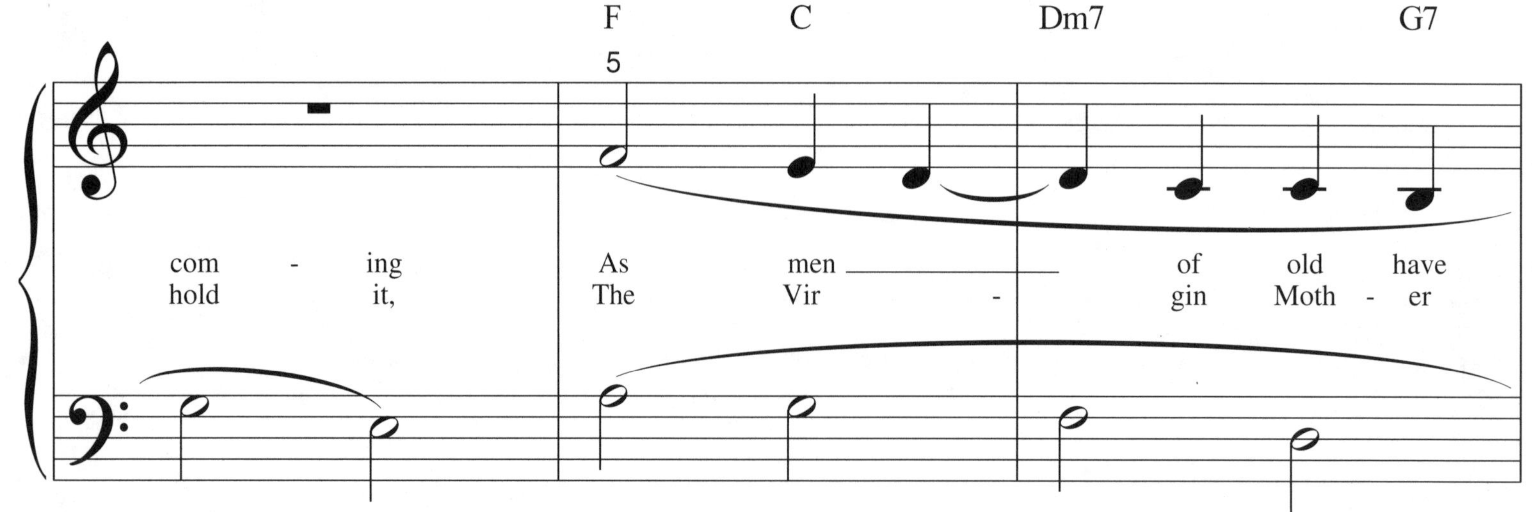

C Bm C D G N.C.
sung. It came, a flow'r - et bright, A -
kind. To show God's love a - right. She
mf
F C
mid the cold of win - ter, When half
bore to men a Sav - ior, When half
Dm7 G7
1. C N.C.
2. C
spent was the night. I -
spent was the night.
mp
F C Dm7 G7 C
p
pp

O CHRISTMAS TREE

Traditional German Carol
Arranged by Phillip Keveren

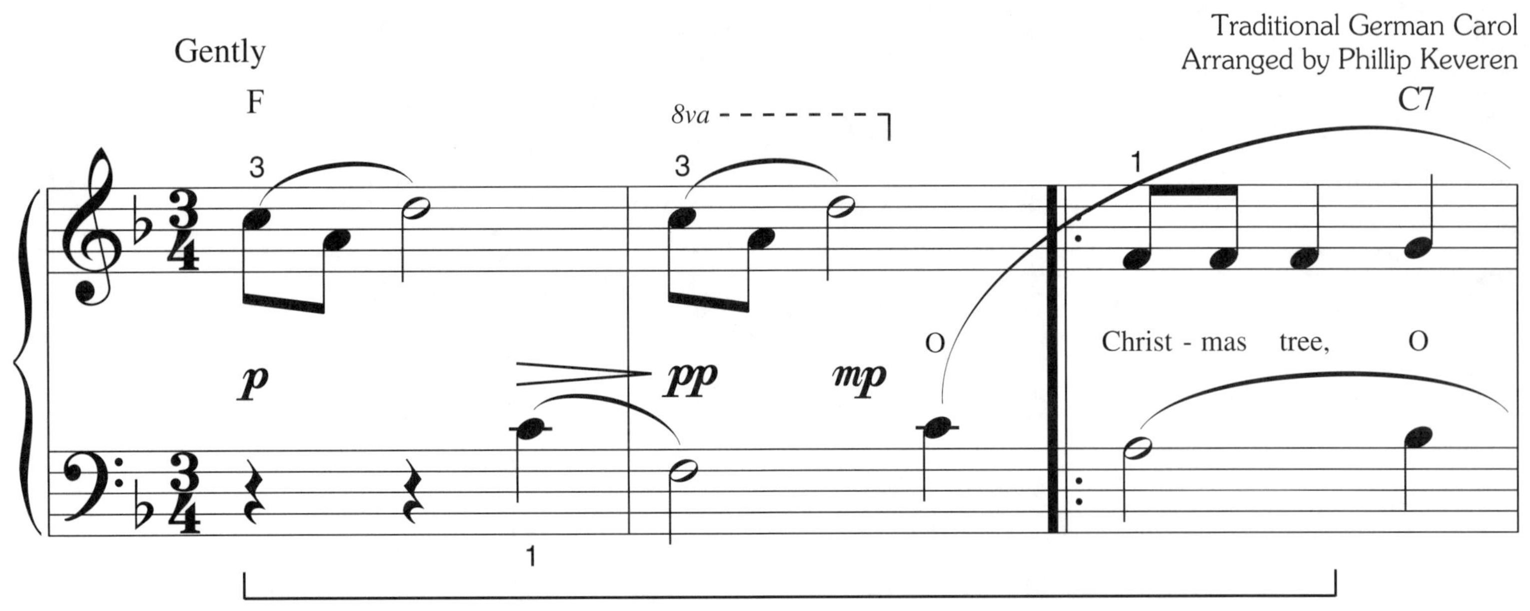

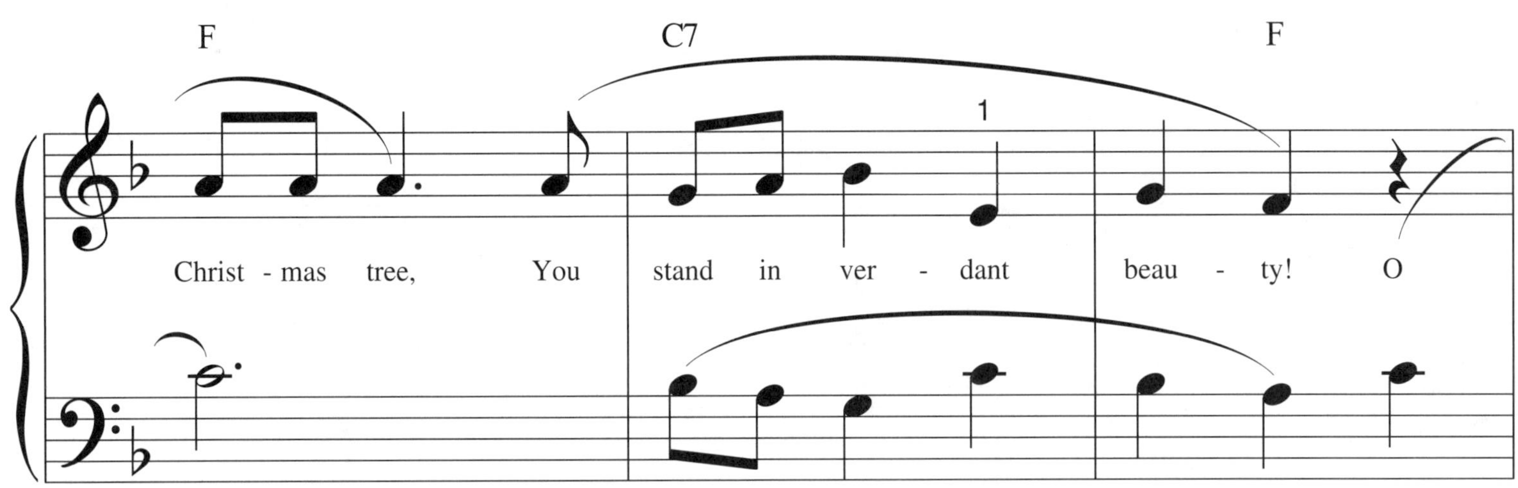

F
Gm7
beau - ty! Your boughs are green in sum - mer's glow, And
mf
C7
F
C7
do not fade in win - ter's snow. O Christ - mas tree, O
mp
F
C7
F
1.
Christ - mas tree, You stand in ver - dant beau - ty!
p
8va
pp
mp
O
2.
8va
15ma
p
pp
rit.
ppp

O COME, ALL YE FAITHFUL

(Adeste Fideles)

Words and Music by JOHN FRANCIS WADE
Latin Words translated by FREDERICK OAKELEY
Arranged by Phillip Keveren

D Em Am D G
Born the King of an - gels;
in the high - est.
O come let us a -
p
dore Him, O come let us a - dore Him, O
D G
mp
mf
D7 G D A7 D D7 G C G/D D7
come let us a - dore Him, Christ the
f
1. G
Lord.
(mp)
2. G G/D D7 G
Lord.
f molto rit.

O COME, O COME, EMMANUEL

Plainsong, 13th Century
Words translated by JOHN M. NEALE and HENRY S. COFFIN
Arranged by Phillip Keveren

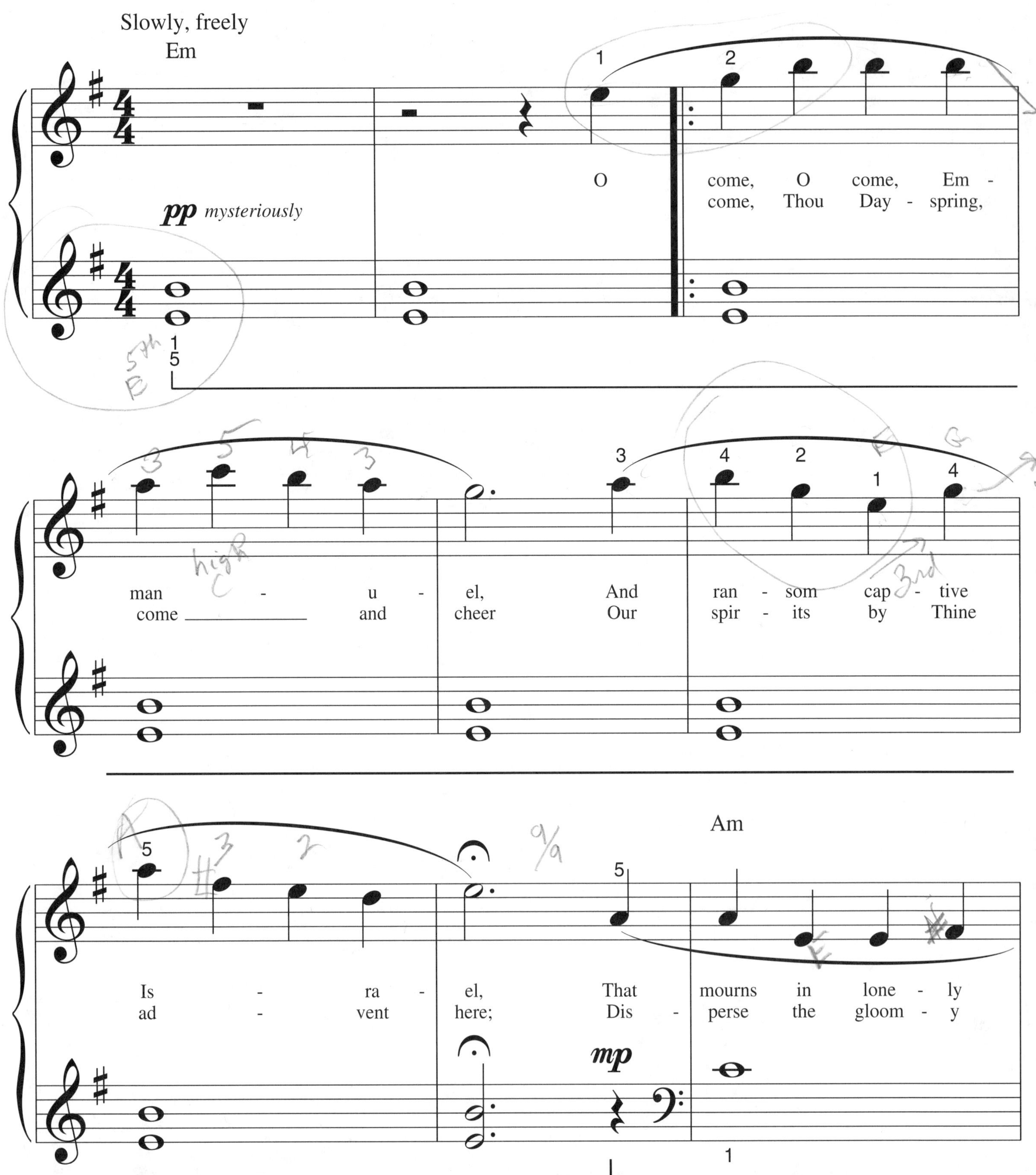

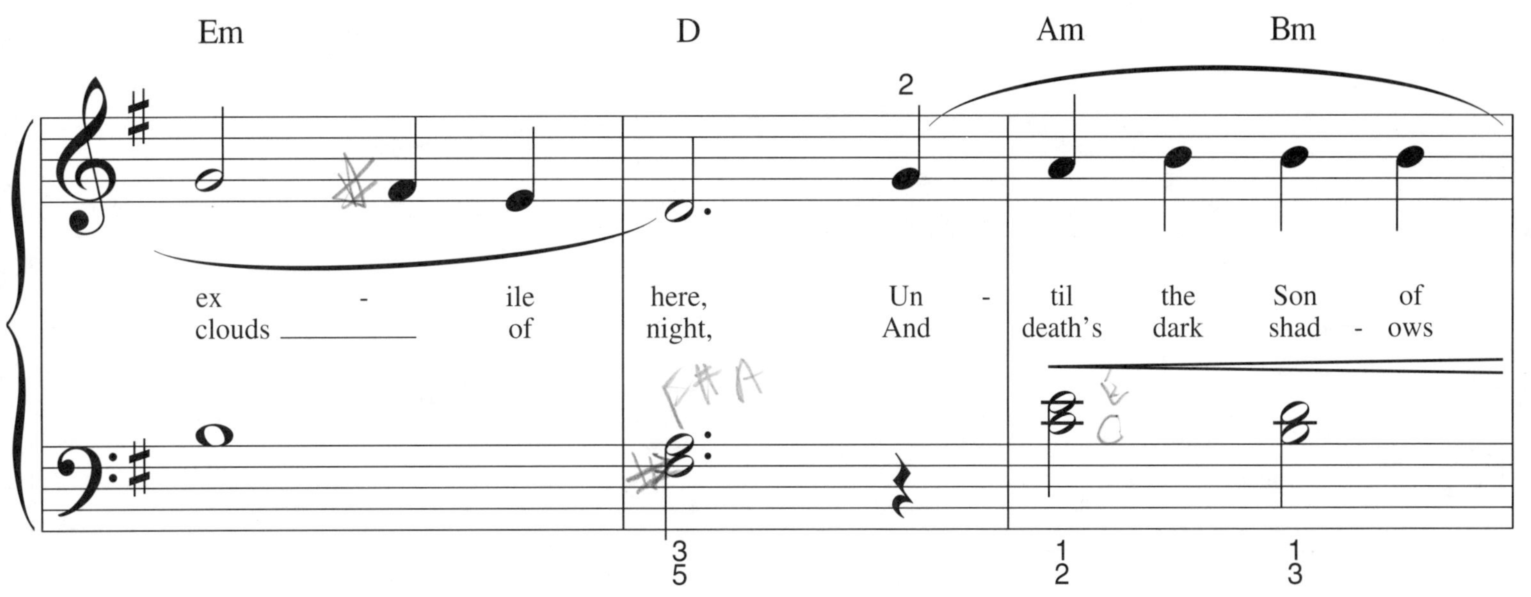
Em
D
Am
Bm
ex - ile here, Un - til the Son of
clouds of night, And death's dark shad - ows

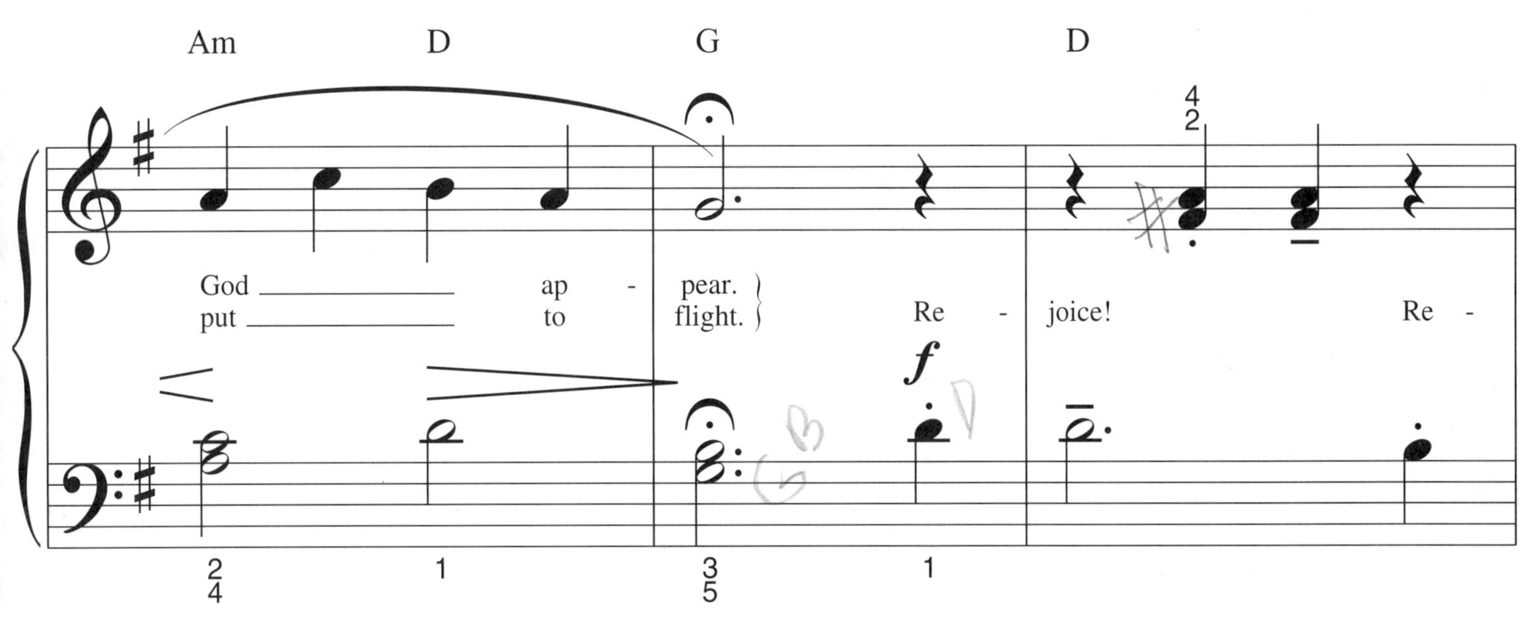
Am
D
G
D
God ap - pear.
put to flight.
Re - joice! Re -

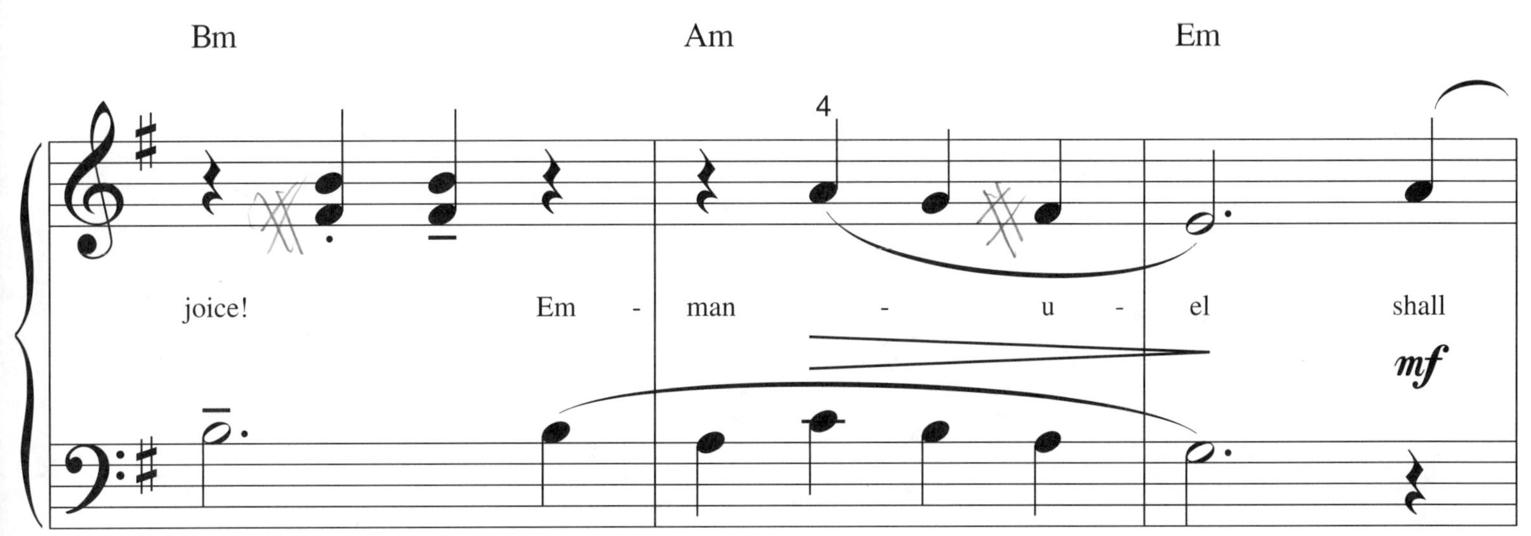
Bm
Am
Em
joice! Em - man - u - el shall

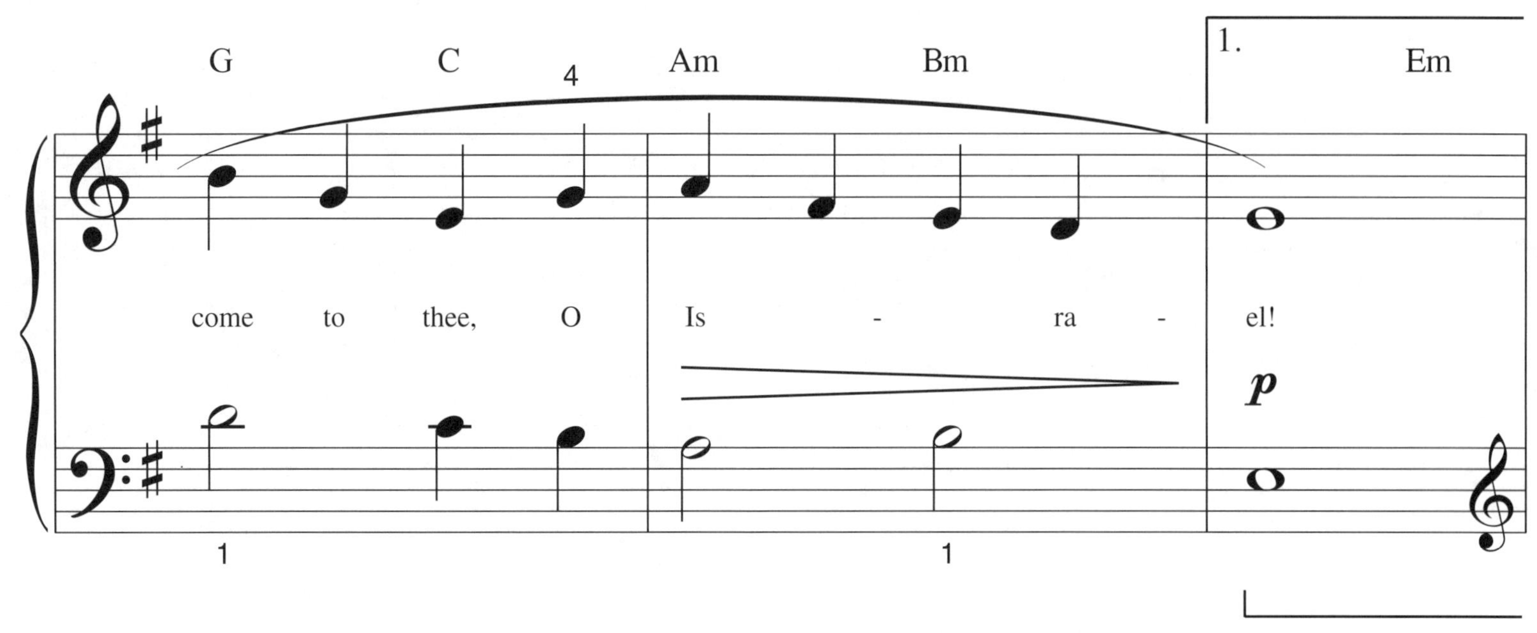
G
C
Am
Bm
1.
Em
come to thee, O Is - ra - el!

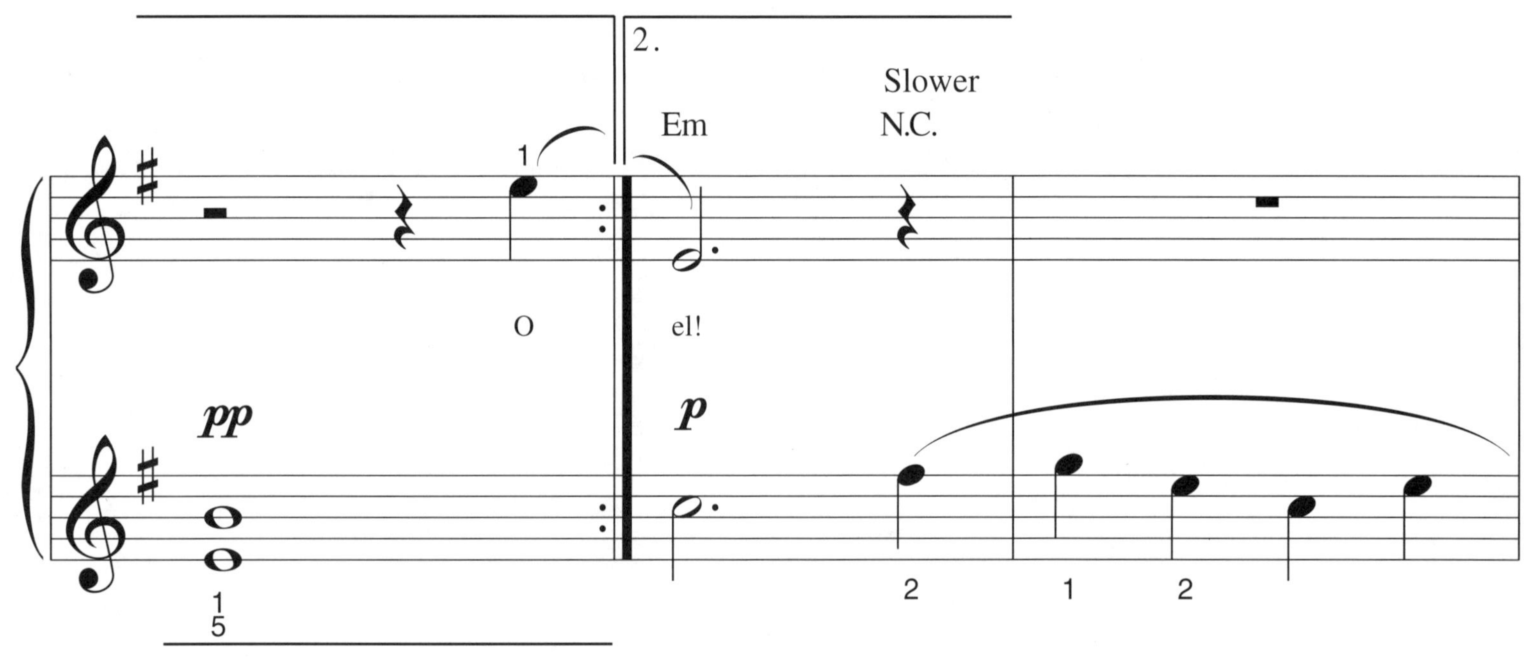
2.
Slower
Em
N.C.
O
el!

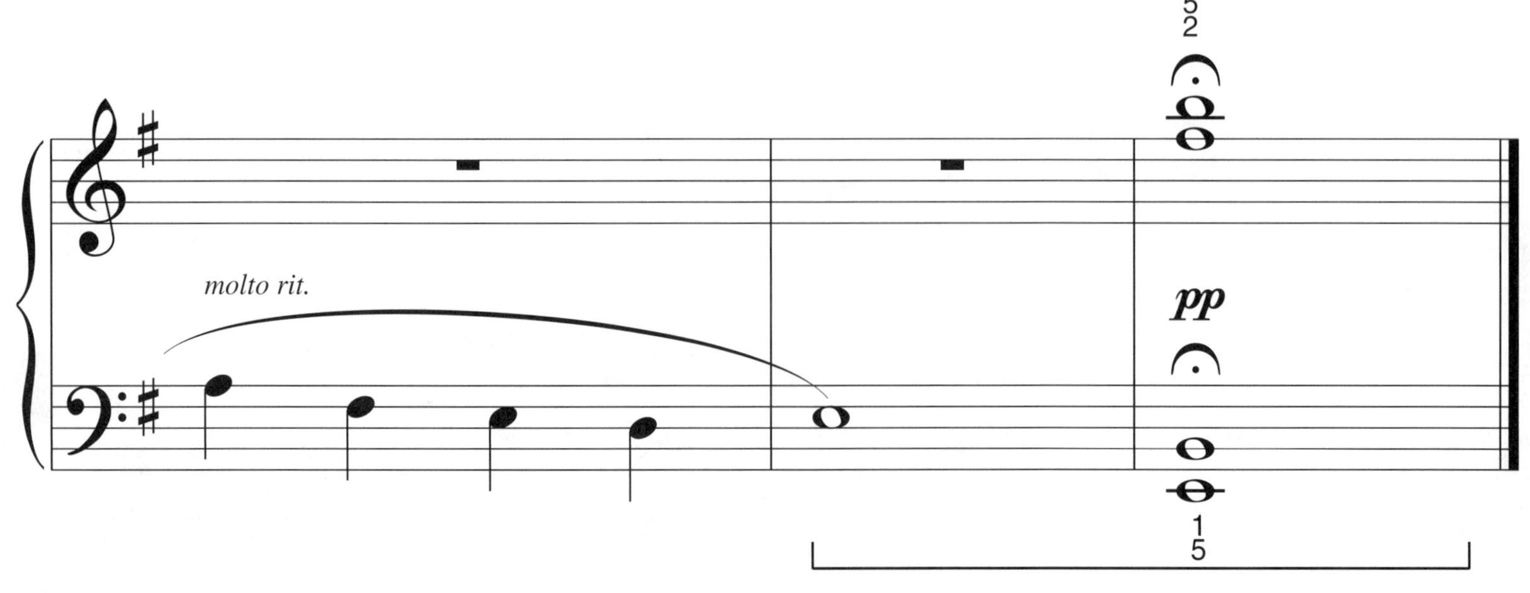
Em(sus2)
molto rit.

SILENT NIGHT

Words by JOSEPH MOHR
Translated by JOHN F. YOUNG
Music by FRANZ X. GRUBER
Arranged by Phillip Keveren

G
G♯dim
Am
F♯m7♭5
C
Sleep in heav - en - ly peace,
Sleep in
mp cresc.
mf
p
G7
Csus
C
Am7
D7
heav - en - ly peace.
cresc.
G
Si - lent night, ho - ly night,
mf
D7
G
Shep - herds quake at the sight.

C
G
Glo - ries stream from heav - en a - far,
p
C
C♯dim
G/D
Heav'n - ly hosts sing al - le - lu - ia;
mp
D
D♯dim
Em
C♯m7♭5
Christ the Sav - ior is born!
mf cresc.
f
rit.
Very slowly
G
D7
Gsus
G
Christ the Sav - ior is born!
p
pp

O HOLY NIGHT

French Words by PLACIDE CAPPEAU
English Words by JOHN S. DWIGHT
Music by ADOLPHE ADAM
Arranged by Phillip Keveren

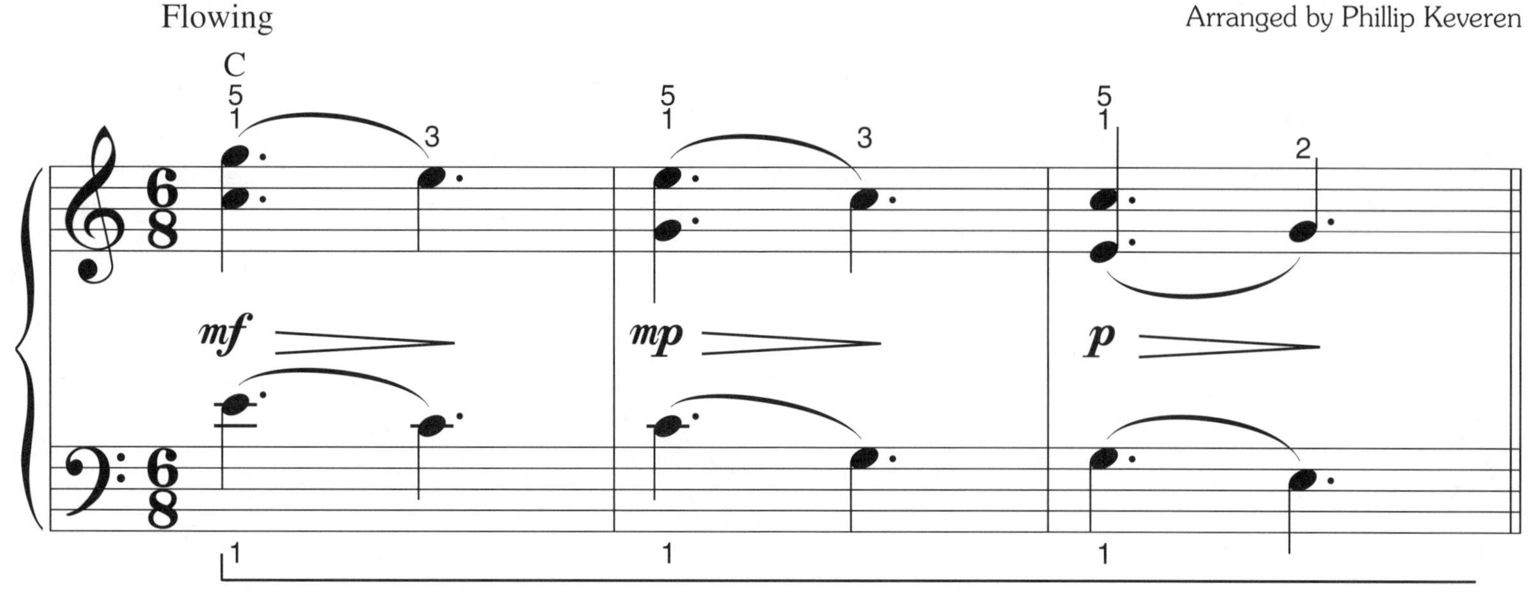

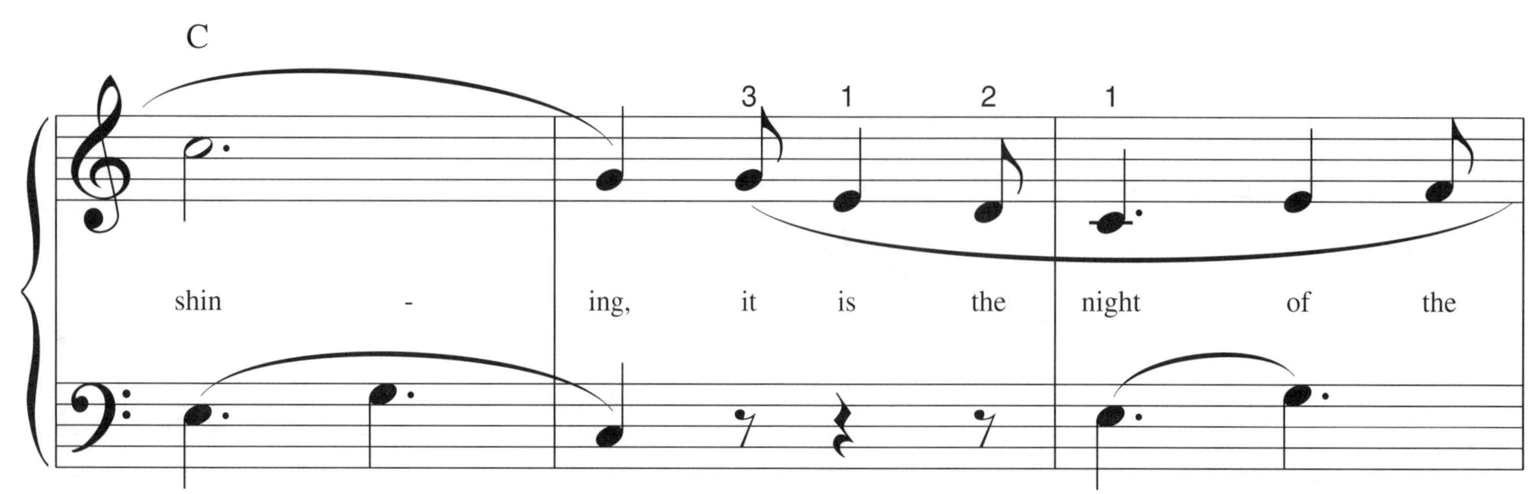

G7
C
1
dear Sav - ior's birth.
Long lay the
F
C
2
world in sin and er - ror pin -
Em
B7
3
4
ing Till He ap - peared and the soul felt its
5
Em
G7
2
1
2
worth. A thrill of hope the
p
2

C
G7
wea - ry world re - joic - es, For yon - der breaks a
mp
C
Am
new and glo - rious morn; Fall on your
mf
Em
Dm
knees! O hear the an - gel
Am
C/G
G
voic - es! O night di -
f

C
F
C
4
vine!
O
night
5
2
4
5
1
G
C
3
when Christ was
born,
O
2
4
1
3
G
C
F
1
5
night
di
-
vine!
O
cresc.
ff rit.
1
2
1
4
G7
C
5
1
night,
O
night
di
-
vine!
molto rit.
1
5
1
5
1
2
1

O LITTLE TOWN OF BETHLEHEM

Words by PHILLIPS BROOKS
Music by LEWIS H. REDNER
Arranged by Phillip Keveren

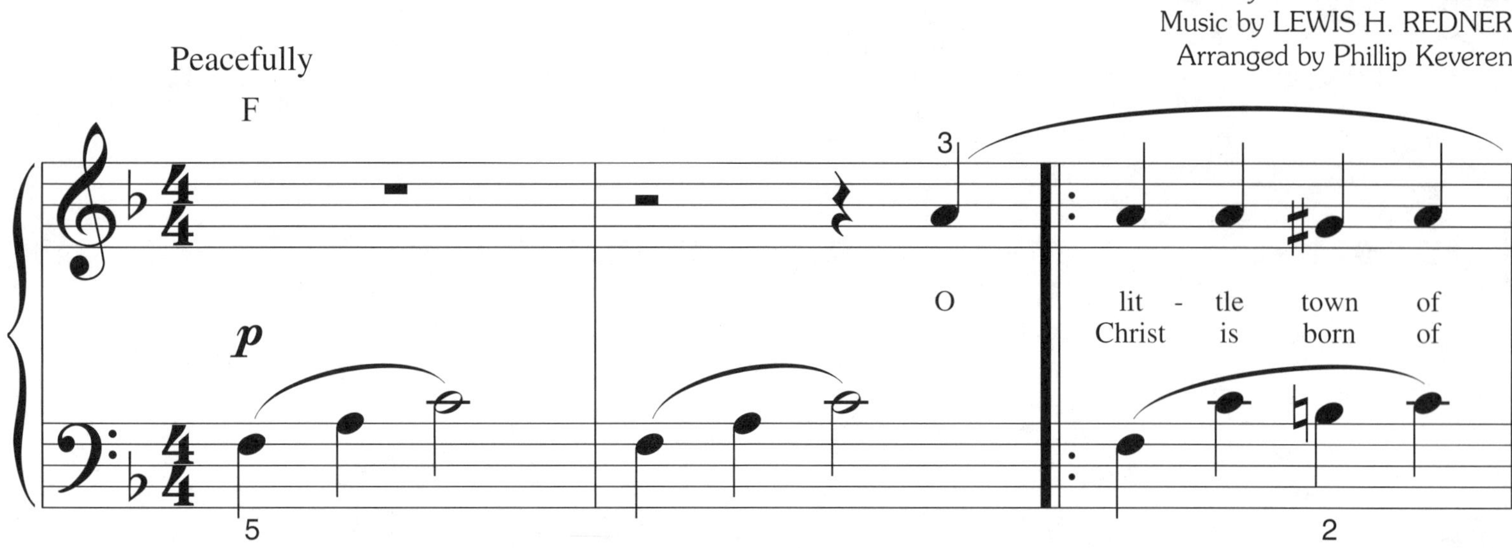

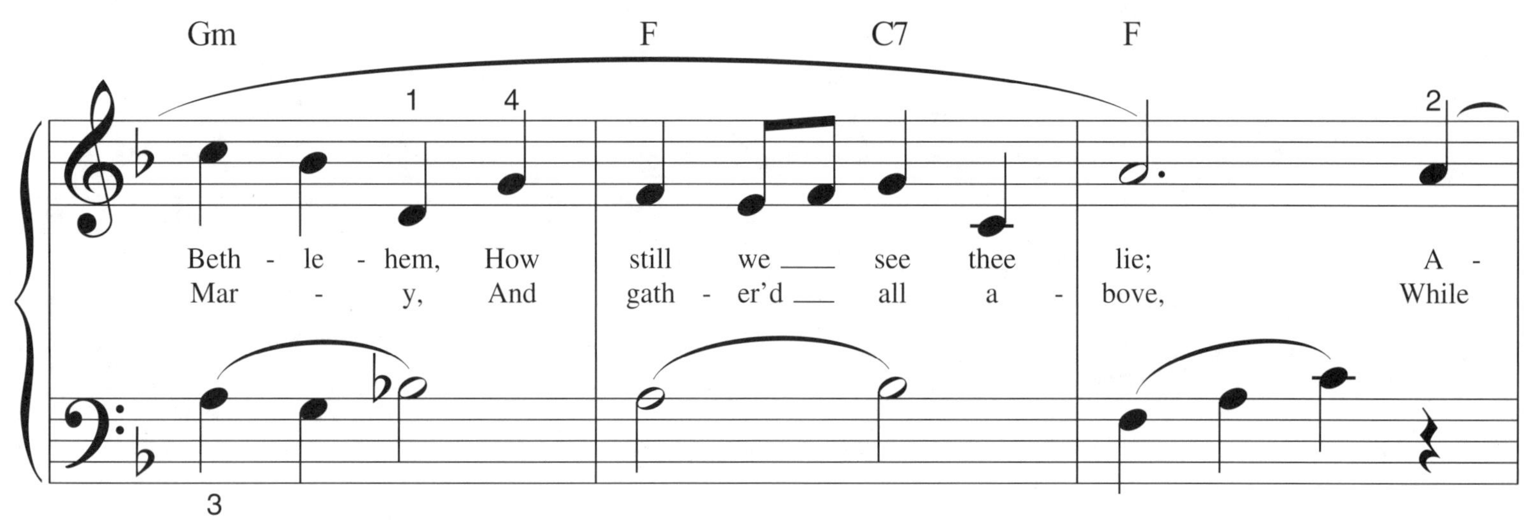

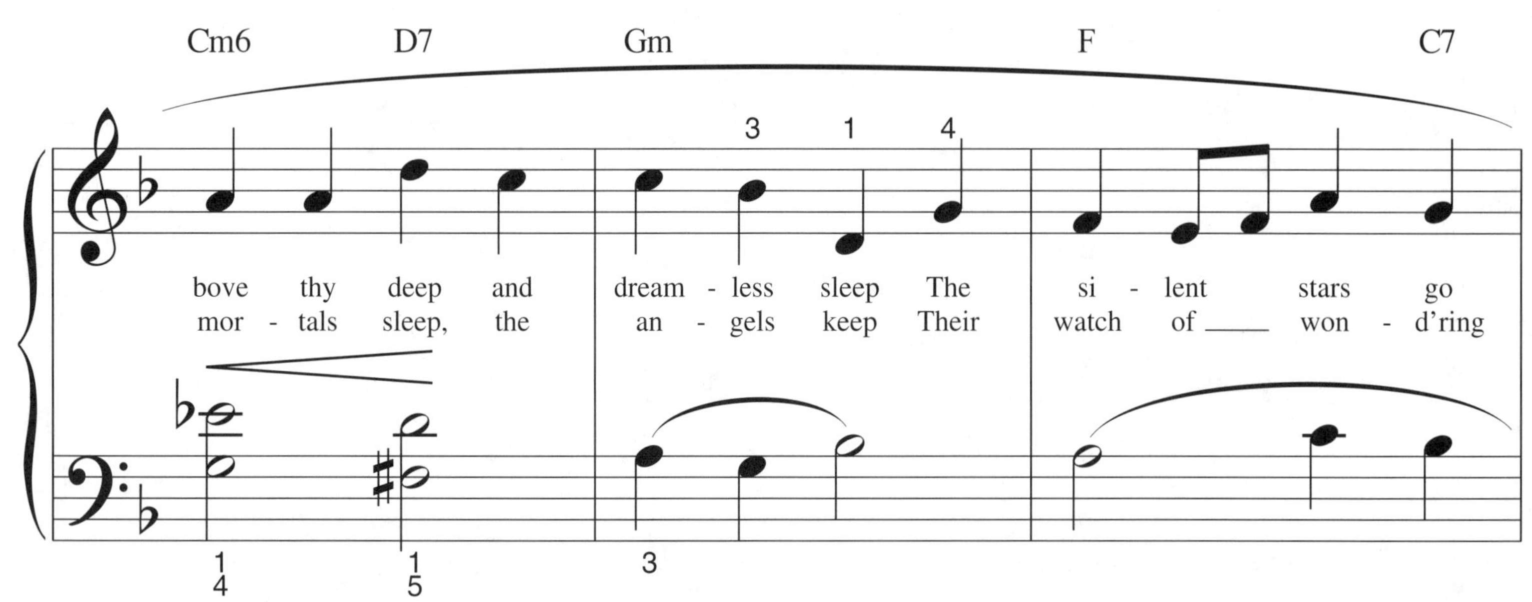

F
Gm Gdim A
by. Yet in thy dark streets shin - eth The
love. O morn - ing stars, to - geth - er Pro -
mf
Dm A F
ev - er - last - ing light; The hopes and fears of
claim the ho - ly birth! And prais - es sing to
f
mf
Gm
1. F C7 F
all the years Are met in thee to - night. For
God the King, And
p
2. F C7 F
peace to men on earth!
p

WE THREE KINGS OF ORIENT ARE

Words and Music by JOHN H. HOPKINS, JR.
Arranged by Phillip Keveren

Slowly, steadily

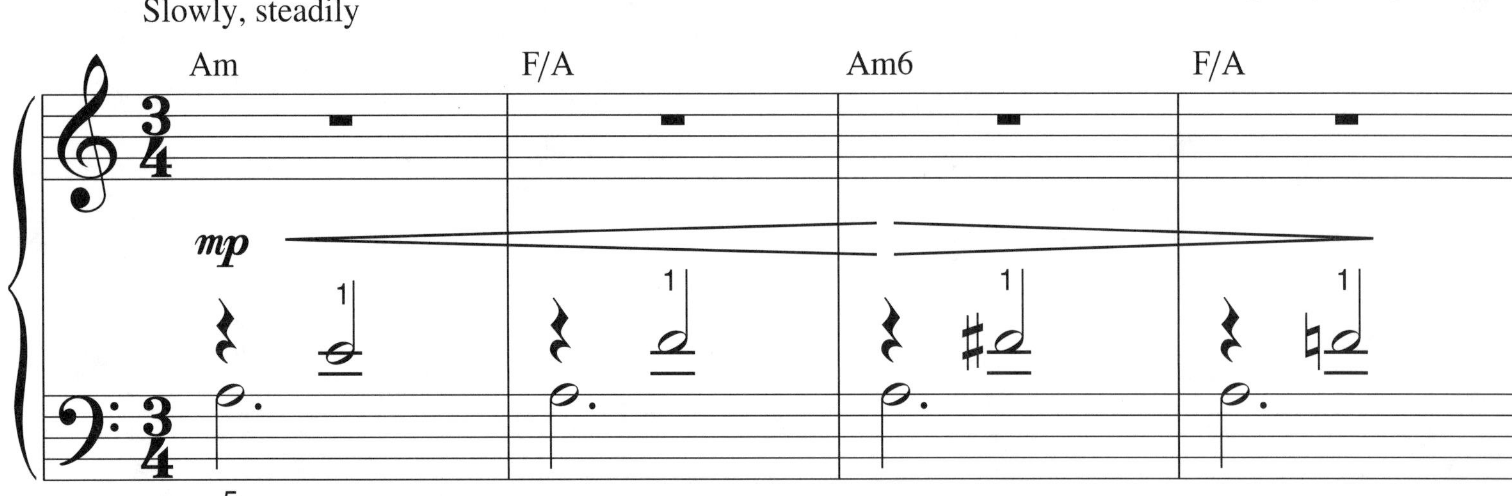

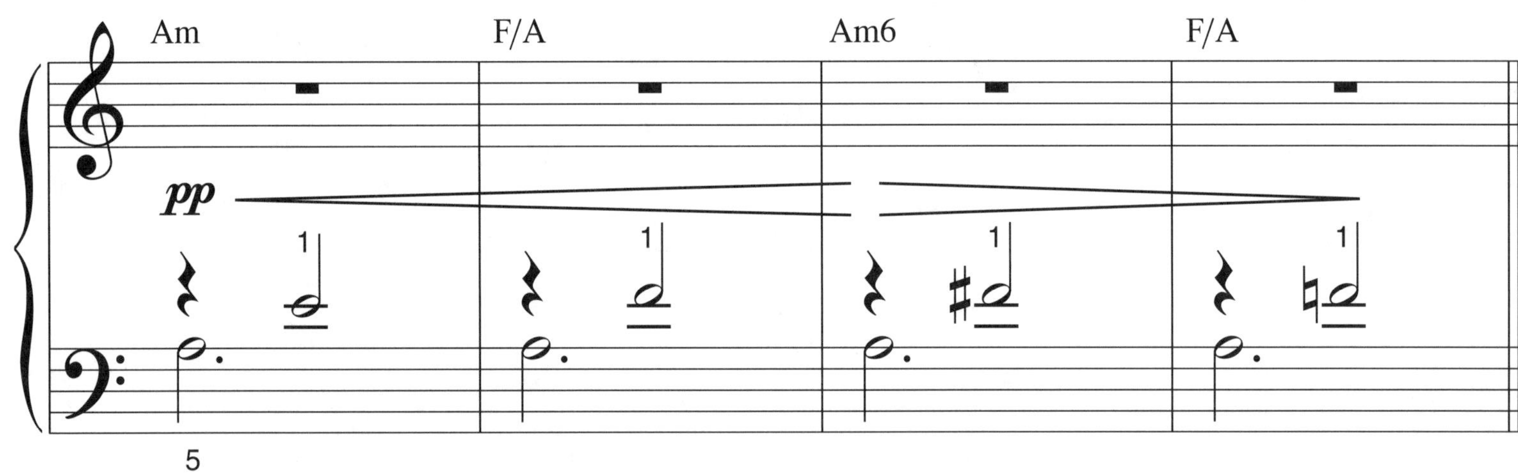

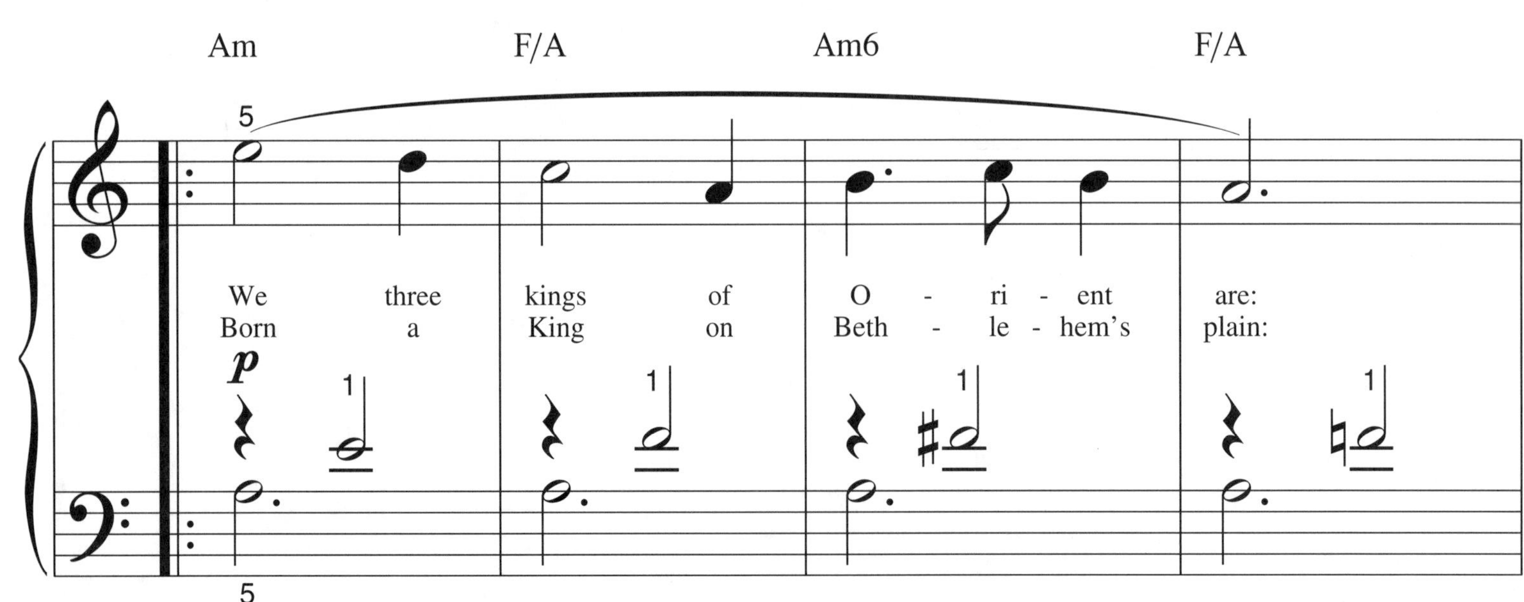

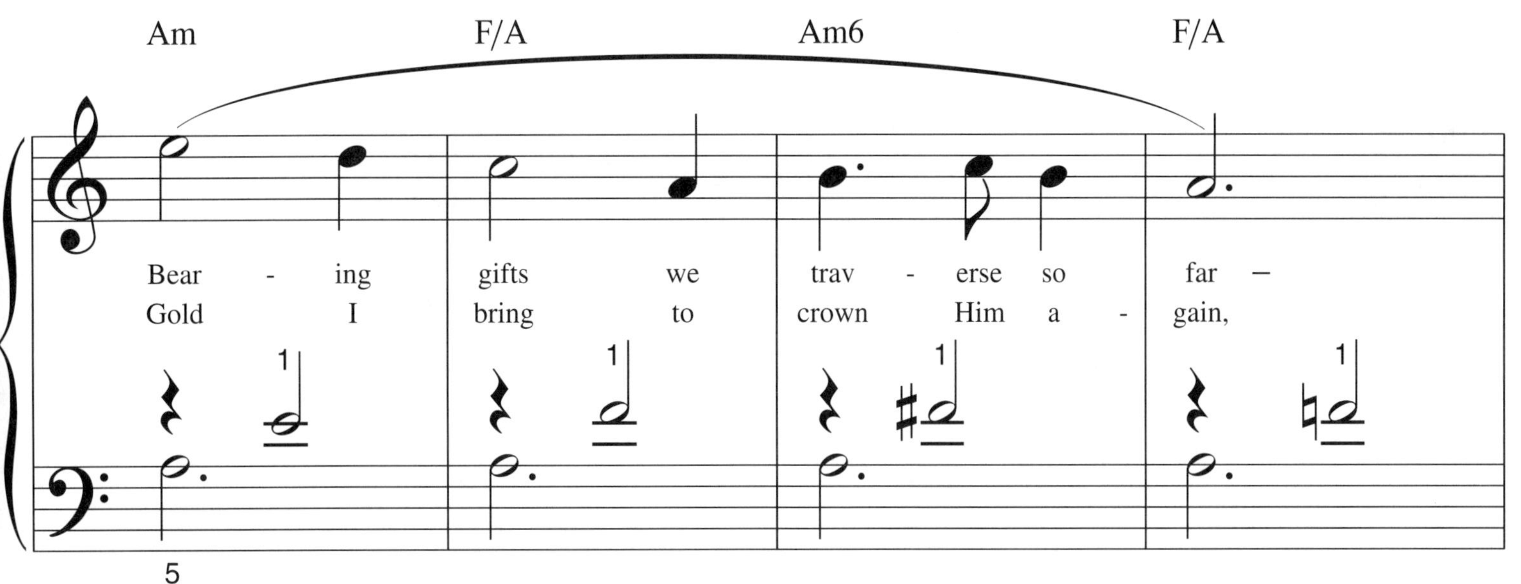
Am
F/A
Am6
F/A
Bear - ing gifts we trav - erse so far —
Gold I bring to crown Him a - gain,
1
1
1
1
5

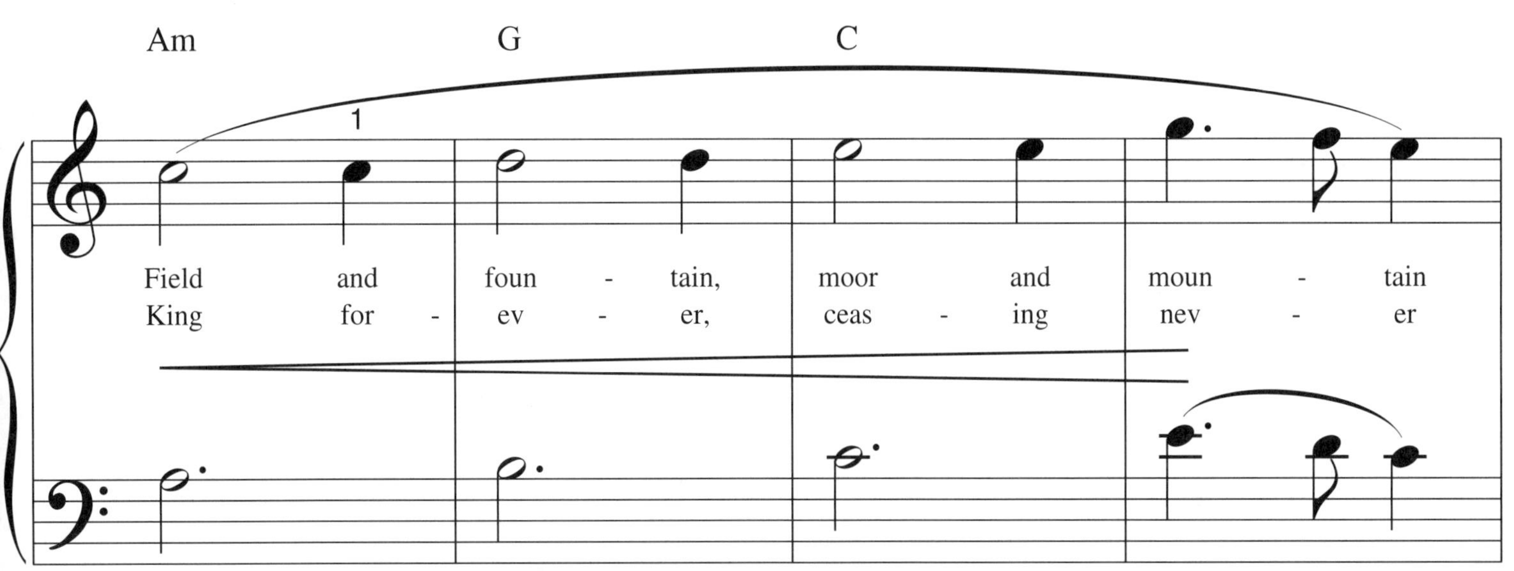
Am
G
C
1
Field and foun - tain, moor and moun - tain
King for - ev - er, ceas - ing nev - er

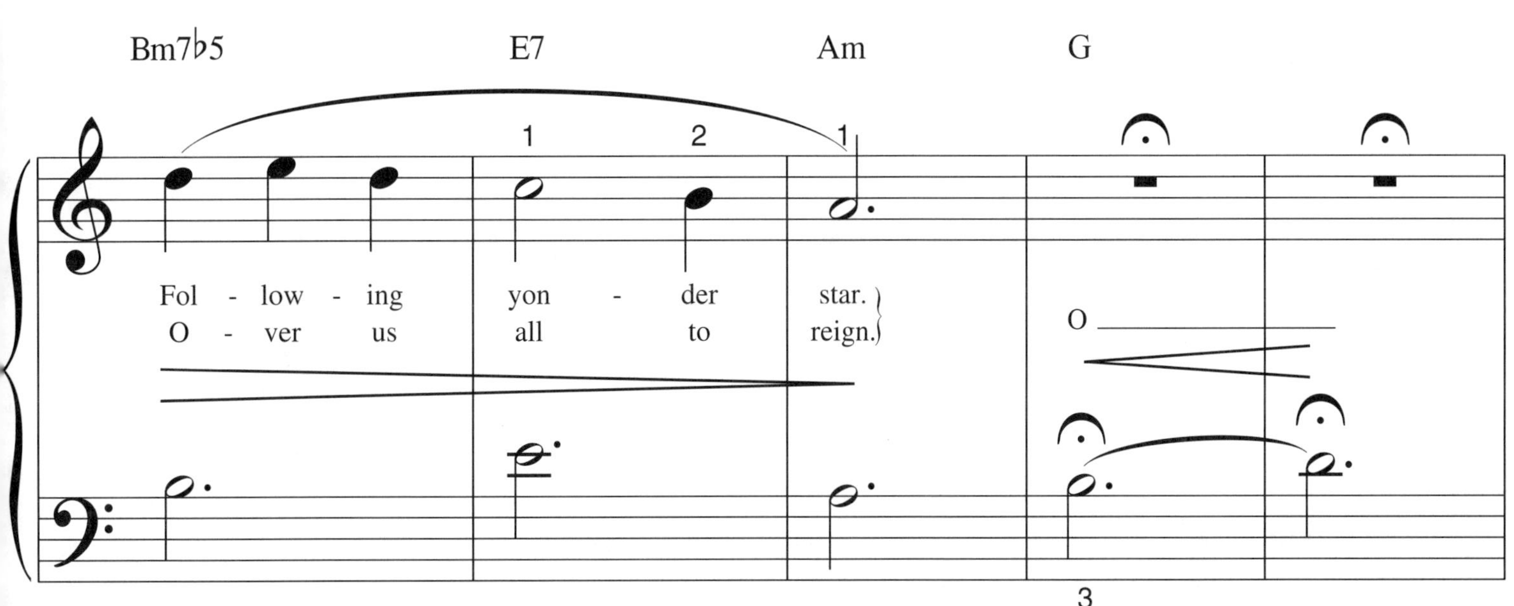
Bm7♭5
E7
Am
G
1
2
1
Fol - low - ing yon - der star.
O - ver us all to reign.
O
3

C
F
star of won - der, star of
mf
C
F
night, Star with roy - al beau - ty
C
Am
G
C
F
C
bright, West - ward lead - ing, still pro -
cresc.
G
C
F
ceed - ing, Guide us to thy per - fect
f
rit.

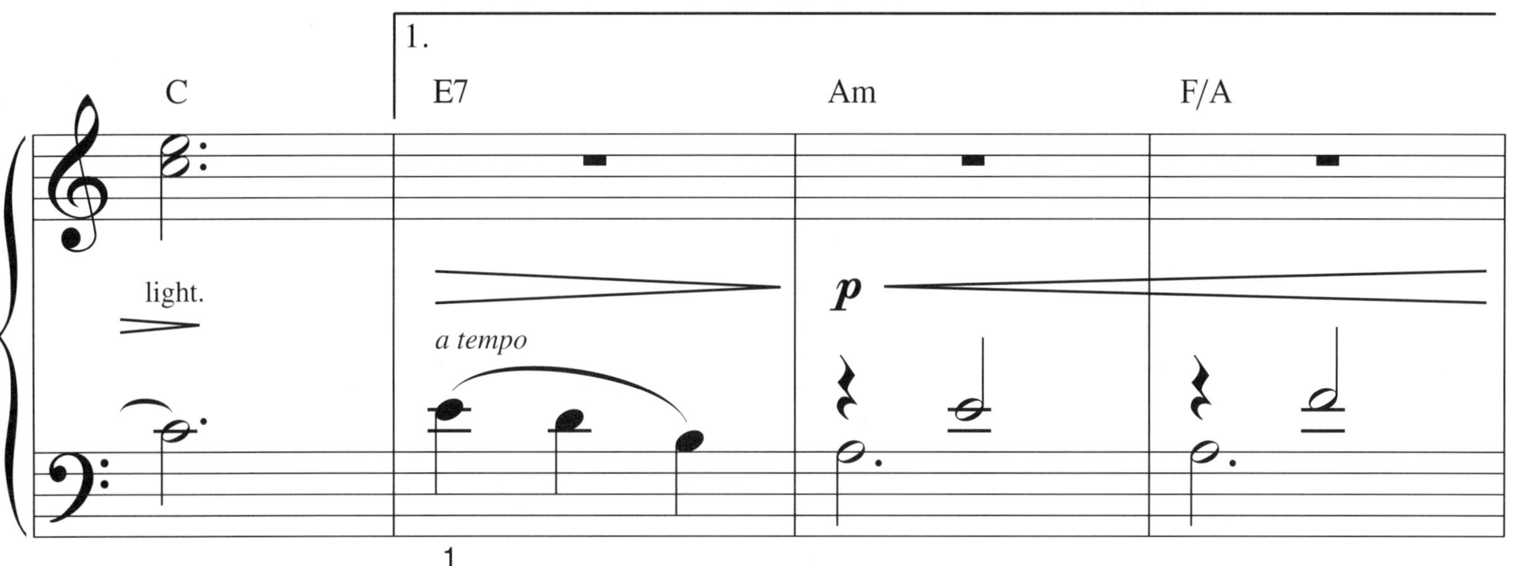
1.
C
E7
Am
F/A
light.
a tempo
p
1

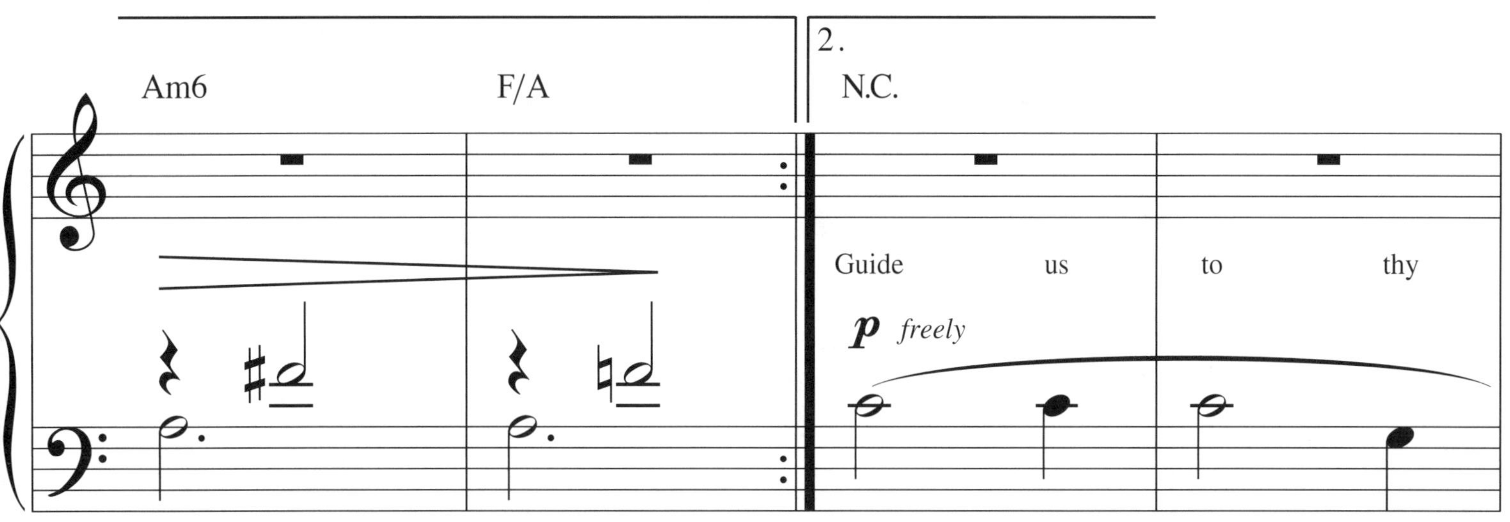
2.
Am6
F/A
N.C.
Guide us to thy
p freely

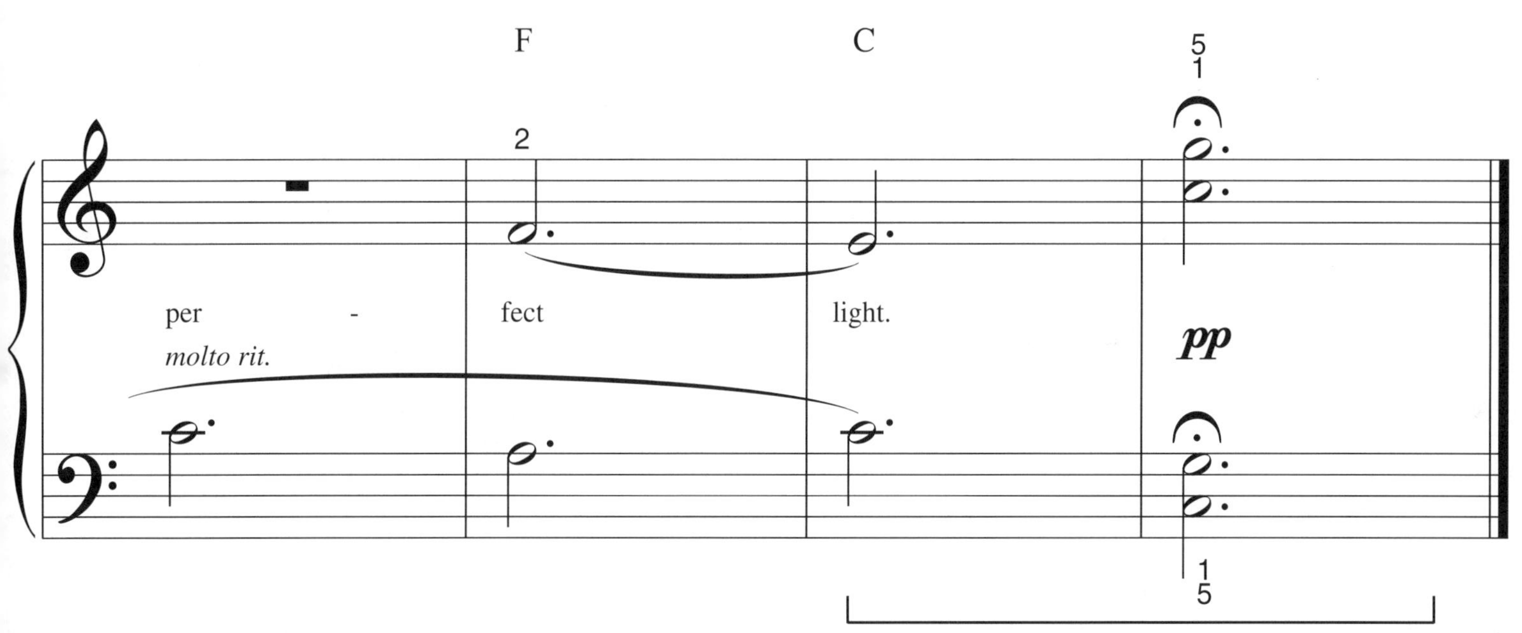
F
C
5
1
2
per - fect light.
molto rit.
pp
1
5

WHAT CHILD IS THIS?

Words by WILLIAM C. DIX
16th Century English Melody
Arranged by Phillip Keveren

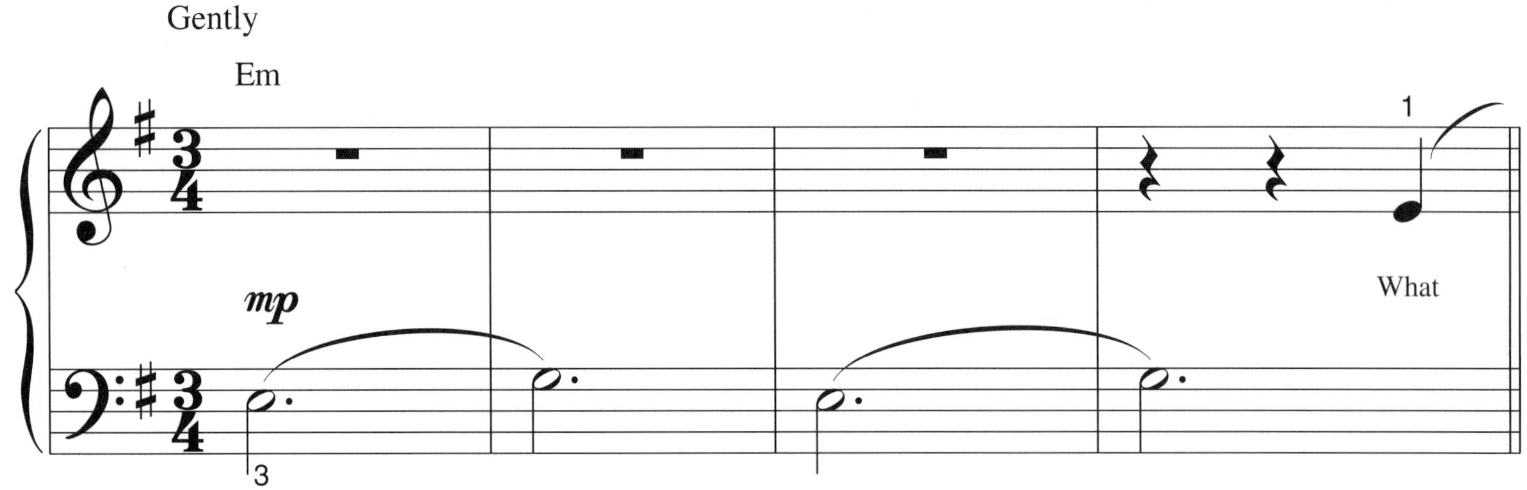

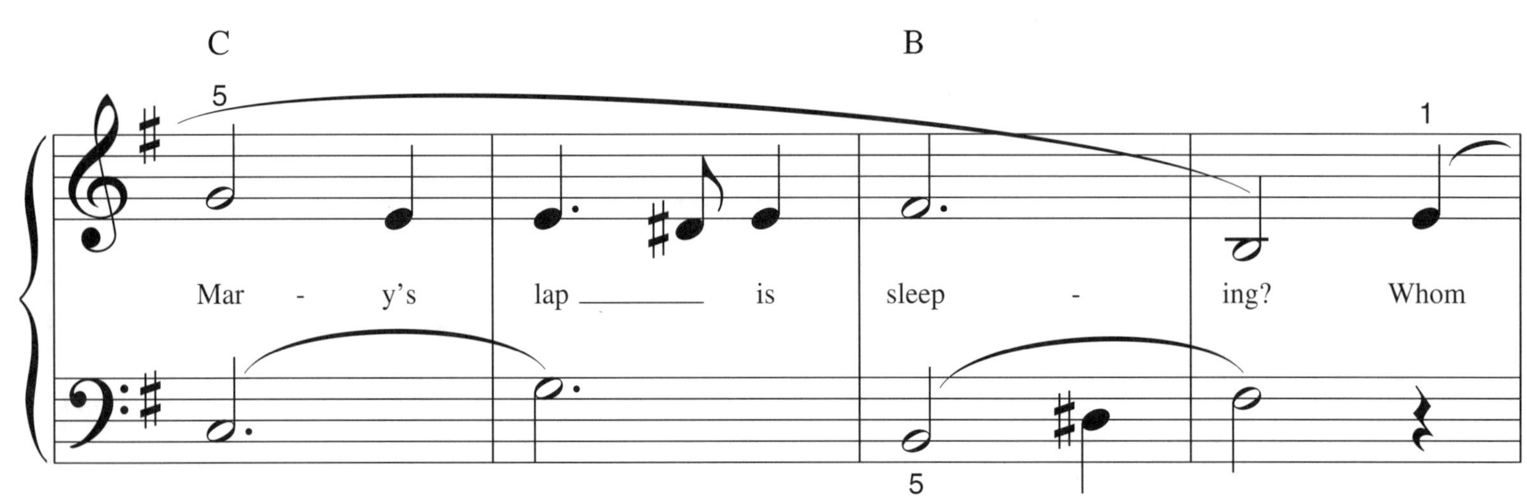

Em
D
an - gels greet with an - thems sweet while
C
B7
Esus
Em
shep - herds watch are keep - ing?
G
D
This, this is Christ, the King, Whom
mf
Em
B7
shep - herds guard and an - gels sing;

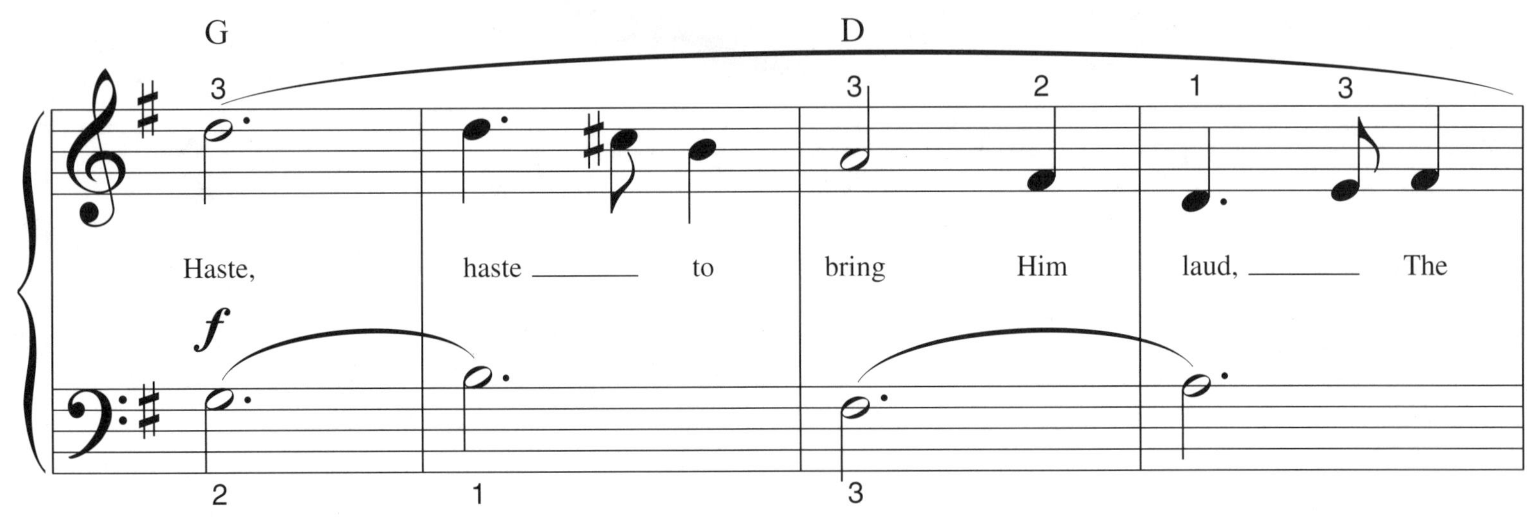
G
D
Haste, haste to bring Him laud, The
f

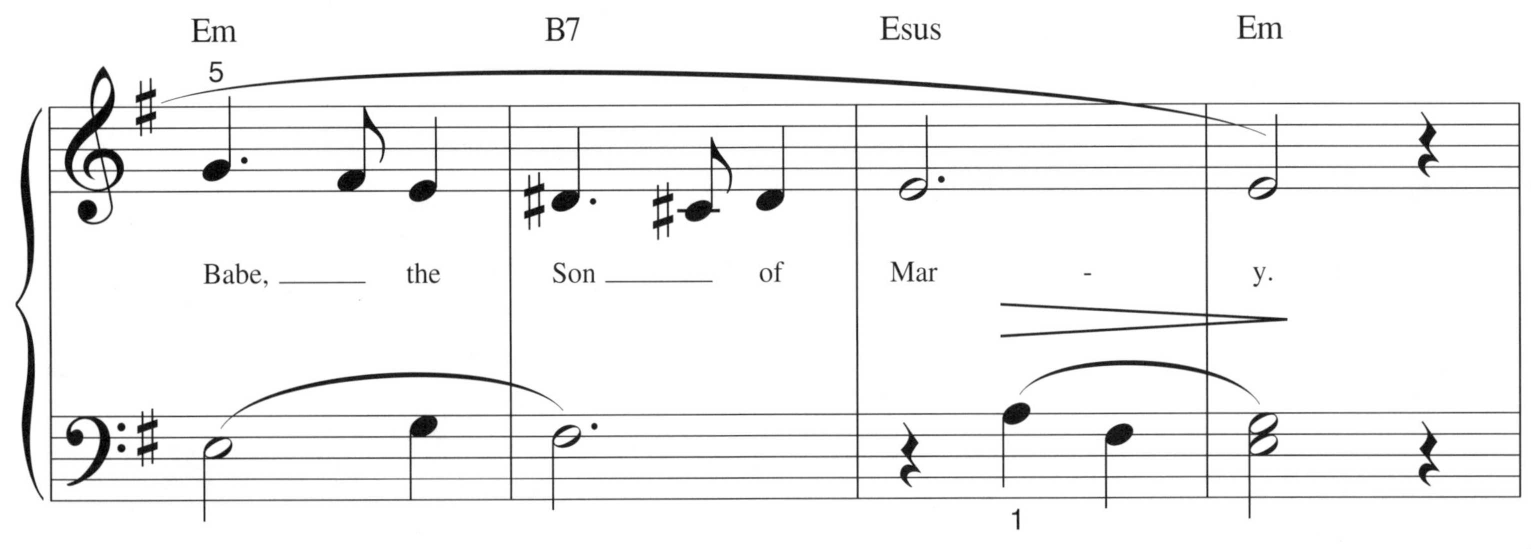
Em
B7
Esus
Em
Babe, the Son of Mar - y.

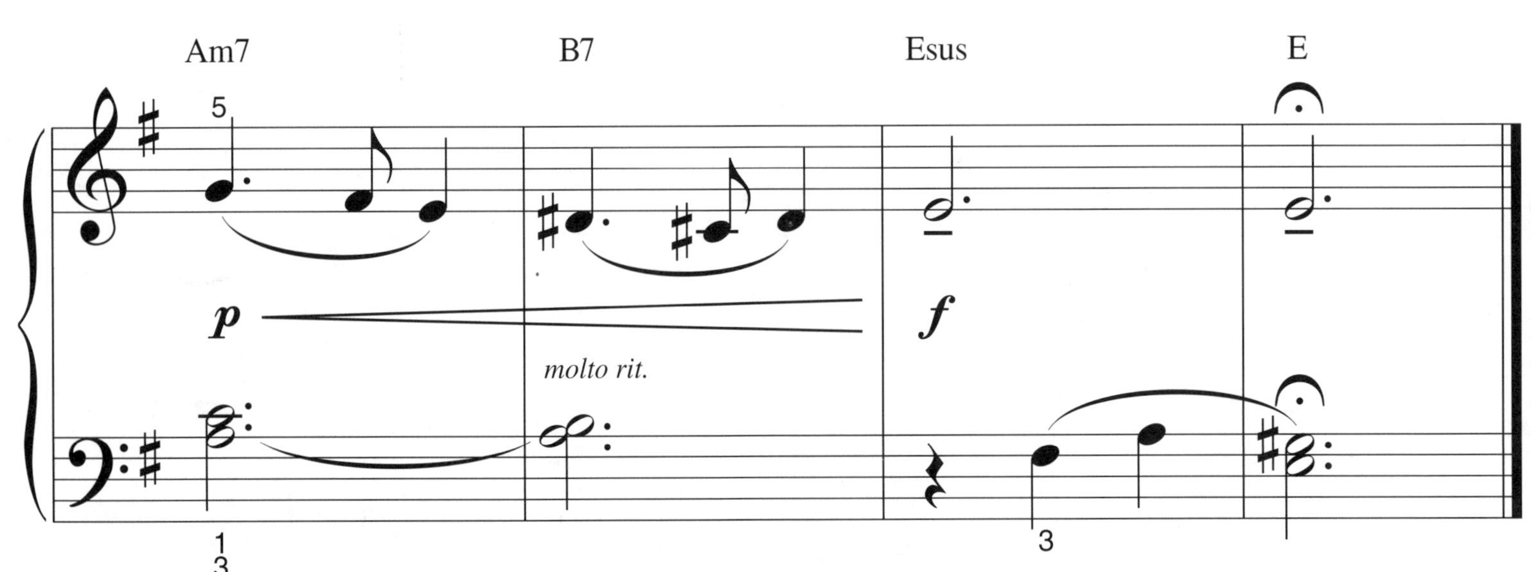
Am7
B7
Esus
E
p
molto rit.
f